I0471286

Private Equity Can:

Make the Large$t
Fortune$ Ever
& BILLIONS of PEOPLE HAPPY

Private Equity Can:

MAKE THE LARGE$T FORTUNE$ EVER & BILLIONS OF PEOPLE HAPPY

Terrence McCloy

Copyright 2013 by Terrence McCloy. Published 2013.
ISBN: 1492355917
ISBN 13: 9781492355915
Printed in the United States of America
Published with CreateSpace.com

To my late, great parents and brother.

To business people and the prosperity that they create with their employees.

ACKNOWLEDGMENT

The staff at Amazon.com's CreateSpace have been a great help in publishing this book. Terrific people, great organization.

CONTENTS

PREFACE

I sought to write perhaps the best business disruptor book ever, in finance, in the sports business, in education, in personal robots. Apologies in advance to readers for whom the book is not that. At least the book is inexpensive. A major player in business could send the book to counterparts for response and make some popular business history.

Fun Disruptor Chapter One
THE BIGGEST CHANGE IN THE WORLD THAT SMARTPHONES CAN MAKE

In 1990 there were one billion people in the world who could make discretionary purchases. Now, there are two billion and growing. Given the opportunity, they might like to make purchases across national borders and across oceans.

Consider that, say, Switzerland announced that it would issue a new, online-only, smartphone-only, digital-only, worldwide currency, called the Zurich. Issued by 'Swiss Global Bank' via a free download of 'Zurichs' to two billion smartphone owners. The 'Zurich' is for cross-border, online purchases only. And, using 'Swiss Global Bank' currency conversion, every seller worldwide is to be paid only in their home-country currency.

The 'Zurich' would allow international, notably trans-ocean, smartphone purchases among 2,000,000,000 to 3,000,000,000 individuals and businesses, with a universal, online currency common denominator. One result could be a large disintermediation of a huge world of cargo ships, warehouses, distributors, wholesalers and retailers.

There could be disintermediation of container ships. The modern container ships are a vast improvement over the old, stevedores era. Some of the largest ships carry 18,000 containers. Yet, each one of these containers needs to be packed up, loaded onto a truck and then loaded onto the ship, then, at destination port, unloaded, its contents transshipped by train and truck, and then unpacked, and then the contents trucked to warehouses or to individual stores. These are expensive tasks. They are not without damage and pilferage.

Shipping from, say, Hong Kong or Rio de Janeiro or Paris by FedEx or UPS to the individual, online buyer in the U.S. or wherever is not necessarily more expensive than truck to container ship to truck to warehouse to truck to the back of the retail store to the front of the retail store to the paid store clerk selling to the individual buyer.

In many instances, UPS-FedEx may be cheaper. Especially in the case of perishables. Fifty per cent of flowers wilt and cannot be sold. In contrast, consider a Valentine's Day buyer in San Diego. He goes online directly to the grower-sellers, in Chile and Israel. The flower gardener shows to him, on Skype, forty-eight beautiful, long-stem roses. The buyer says, "One of those roses looks a bit wilted." The seller immediately removes that rose and sticks in a new one.

How much are the 48 gorgeous roses? Equivalent to ten U.S. dollars. "Ten Zurichs," says the seller. Plus FedEx or UPS. Sold.

In this example, the 'Zurich', would be 'The World Exchange'.

It is worth mentioning in passing that Zurich as the name of an online-only, world currency, rather than a lovely Swiss city, would be a bad choice. The reasons are three. First, Zurich has two syllables. Currency names with two syllables get shortened in popular use to one syllable slang. The dollar becomes the buck. The pound becomes the quid.

Second, the word Zurich may need an 's' for the plural. "I bet you ten Zurichs that Manchester United wins...."

Third, any name of a world, online currency should not be one nation or culture or bank imposing its own local loyalties and preferences or fads on the rest of the world. A universal name is called for. Nor should the name be cute or lovable. To billions of people, money is daily, serious stress. It ain't for fun. Thus, no to currency names such as Love, or Green, or Peace, or Beauty, or Kitten, or Mao, or Sex, or Pot. Sorry!

A Group of Major Players Become Heroes to the World

The most trusted, online-only, private-sector, world currency can be founded and distributed by free, currency-validation, *smartphone downloads to 2,000,000,000 perhaps 3,000,000,000 people, overnight.*

For example, as proposed herein, a group of major players in finance, from five continents, could become heroes to the world.

Consider that one or a few major players, prominent business leaders, from the U.S. and abroad, invite a larger, select group of Major Players to 'critical mass' size, perhaps 25 or so Major Players, to a 'Money Summit'. Such a summit could be held anywhere, but say for the purposes here, held perhaps in Beijing. Or Singapore or Wellington or Dublin or the City of London.

What of national governments and their concerns that governments alone issue currency? Payments in the new, additional, online-only currency would proactively be only in the seller's home-currency. The seller may list his or her wares in the universal, online currency, while still being paid in the seller's home-currency, via the proposed World Treasury Bank MAiNPay *Intrabank Conversion.*

The new, online-only, digital-only, private-sector, international-only currency is proactively an *additional* currency only, *not a replacement* currency. It is not a replacement currency even for the Zimbabwean dollar. That honor belongs to the Botswana pula.

To Illustrate the Point: Consider that some small nation, self-admittedly doing a bad job of running its own currency, asked the new currency bank, World Treasury Bank MAiN, to take over the nation's currency, and run it for the nation.

There is no way on earth, or in space, that the new currency bank would engage in such folly. Consider the nightmare logistics of minting and printing and distributing the currency to every cash drawer and bank and wallet and underneath-the-mattress in the nation. Horrors. Then there is the nightmare problem of counterfeiting.

Yet, the nightmare would only grow because, human folly being what it is, the nation's legislature would never let up in tireless, grim 'suggestions' that the currency be inflated, to cover the usual vast overspending of so many nations. Therefore, no way, no how, not now, not ever, not in any circumstances, not even if our mothers ask us.

To Illustrate the Point: Consider that Wal-Mart (a great corporation in our view, that saves its customers $100 Billion a year), for some reason wanted to arrange to accept MAiN in America or in any other nation.

World Treasury Bank would respond, respectfully, "This is a crazy idea for many reasons. How would change be given for any purchase? Every World Treasury Bank Savings Account holder can effortlessly, in a few seconds, forex their MAiN for the U.S. dollar, or for any other currency. The dollar is the legal currency, legal tender in America. The dollar works great. We love the dollar. The U.S. Treasury will object if you at Wal-Mart try to use another currency. Moreover, World Treasury Bank credit cards and debit cards, just like any other out-of-country credit cards, automatically pay in the home-currency where the retail purchase is made, the dollar alone here in America. Therefore, forget this idea. Stick to the U.S. dollar. USA! USA!"

The MAiN

The proposed name of the online-only, smartphone-only currency is: the MAiN. Its symbol: M}. The two parts of the symbol are available on most every keyboard in the world.

The MAiN is one, solid syllable, that need not be turned into one-syllable slang.

MAiN has the same, solid, attractive meaning in every language on earth. If the word MAiN is translated into another language, when a user asks a friend, "What does the word MAiN mean in English?", he is pleased by the answer.

MAiN keeps the same spelling for single and plural. One MAiN. One million MAiN.

MAiN is likely to be a free-market currency. It would not be tied to any other, nor to a basket of other currencies. This would be to tie MAiN to the folly of legislatures that engage in inflating their currencies. MAiN might be tied to gold.

MAiN is to be inflation-free. This helps billions of people.

The IDEA In One Sentence

World Treasury Bank MAiN is to use current-yet-disruptive, smartphone technology to please literally billions of people in the world by currency-validation distributions via *free*, smartphone downloads worldwide, and by growing international commerce.

An incidental result, to create perhaps, the richest individuals in the world, the Founders of World Treasury Bank MAiN. Richest and world acclaimed like great statesmen. And stateswomen. As seen in the Contents list of this book.

Legislators in a nation, say the People's Republic of China, may ask themselves, 'Is there any disadvantage to us if we let smartphone users in China download a one-time 10,000 free MAiN, then perhaps forex exchange that MAiN to Yuan on the World Treasury Bank site?'. World Treasury Bank MAiN may invite a senior Chinese official to be on the Bank's Board of Directors, perhaps from the National People's Congress or from the Chinese People's Political Consultative Conference.

If the downloaders had earned any money abroad and brought it back to China, that would likely be fine with China. The MAiN currency-validation distribution to 2,000,000,000+ people worldwide helps international trade and each nation's economic vigor. The national legislators in each nation may well consult with Major Players, billionaires in their own nation who are involved in the MAiN issuance.

What if a national legislature decides that for its own reasons, it does not want the MAiN distribution for its smartphone users? That is their choice. No problem. They may change after a period of observing other smartphone users in other nations. World Treasury Bank MAiN will abide by the nation's laws. No problem.

This Produces Greater Prosperity

It is to the advantage of any nation that all of its sellers can suddenly, overnight, add to their online wares being listed in home-currency prices, a universal currency price as well, the MAiN, and thereby sell to 200 nations and states.

World Treasury Bank MAiN can be the Home Page on some smartphones. Other worldwide, major Internet sites can feature their logo click-through on the World Treasury Bank MAiN Home Page. And perhaps place their logo click-through on all 2,000,000,000 to 3,000,000,000 World Treasury Bank MAiN pages. Let's discuss.

Would a universal, additional, digital currency better be issued jointly by 200 national treasuries?

It is difficult to conceive of a worse idea. Because folly is the rule in nations handling even their own currency. The worst of the nations in these regards would engage in ceaseless, relentless, never-give-up, tireless advocacy for inflation, and would vote for inflation, to cover their own spendthrift folly. Inflation is theft from middle-class and poor people in particular. In the instance here, human nature being what it is, feckless or resentful or hostile nations, and nations with hidden agendas, would outvote responsible, conscientious, sober nations. There are many Greeces and Cypruses in the world, nice people all. The responsible, sober, conscientious nations, not so many.

MAiN is not a threat to the value of any currency. Each national currency enjoys autonomy and is master of its destiny.

Reserve Currency Cannot Be Us

World Treasury Bank obviously could never be interested in being a 'reserve currency', or anything like it. The reserve currency is a currencies-of-nations matter. Reserve currencies must negotiate exchange rates with other nations. World Treasury Bank MAiN, a free-market, private-sector currency, has no part of any such thing.

Unlikely as it may seem to some smart people whose judgment we greatly respect, many national legislators will like the new, online-only, additional, private-sector currency. This theme is developed with what may be inviting specificity in later chapters. We want this small book to be perhaps The Most Worthy Financial Book Ever. At least we can give it the old college try.

Worth mentioning in passing, "A paper entitled 'Reserve Accumulation and International Monetary Stability', written by the Strategy, Policy and Review Department of the International Monetary Fund, recommends that the world adopt a global currency called the "Bancor" with a global central bank to administer the currency." The report is dated April 13, 2010. This is a serious proposal in an official document from a powerful, world institution.

It is a disastrously inept idea, based on resentment against America. The U.S. is to give up its economic sovereignty to a large group of nations variously incompetent, and hostile to the U.S. Good luck on that.

Worth noting in passing, 'Bancor', whatever that means, is an inept selection of a name. It is two syllables, one too many. And meaningless. "I bet you 50 Bancors that Manchester United wins the game....."

Perhaps they should call it the Imf or the Zim.

Known Wealth and Probity, Is This You?

Virtually nothing is inevitable, except that a lead weight let go of, will fall down rather than up. Yet, it seems reasonable to predict that a worldwide, private-sector, online-only, serious currency will be issued by serious, gravitas-laden men and women of known wealth and probity. Such a currency can delight some billions of people, if issued properly. That is the subject of this book.

The above-noted offers a treasure trove of material for You-Tube and Facebook and Twitter entrants in the opportunity to apply for very large awards that might be paid out. Fun Disruptor Awards Chapter Thirty.

Fun Disruptor Chapter Two
THEY INTEND TO GIVE AWAY TRILLIONS IN CURRENCY IN SMARTPHONE DOWNLOADS

World Acclaim for World Treasury Bank Founders – for Decades

Herewith the Concise Outline, in a few pages, on what may prove to be "The Next Big Thing". You decide.

As noted, a group of major players in finance and business can hold a Money Summit. A Critical Mass of major players can come together, often by Rolodex. Buy copies of this book. It's inexpensive. Send it to colleagues. Some major players may make themselves known to the others. 'Hey, I'm interested.' The Summit can be held in, say for examples, Beijing or Singapore or Wellington or Dublin, even the City of London.
Some former treasury chiefs may be at the Summit.

The major players can and likely will incorporate World Treasury Bank. However they have made no commitent until the incorporation decision.
World Treasury Bank can decide to issue, *The* Private-Sector World-Currency. Online only. Digital-only.

For example, it is as if some or all of, say, Facebook and Yahoo and LinkedIn and Google and PayPal and Apple iTunes and Twitter, great companies with which we have no connection, *jointly issued* a digital-only currency download to their 1.5 billion accounts worldwide.

This is to be an issuance of an online-currency download app, a *free*, Currency-Validation, smartphone download, to two billion, perhaps **three billion, really pleased people, in 200 nations and states**.

The recipients of the free money may well go viral on Facebook and Twitter. *The world may be abuzz.* The Founders of World Treasury Bank may well be spoken of in 'wow, great, fantastic' terms in many languages in 150+ nations. "These rich guys and rich women are fantastic."

Wall Street Is Happy

It is rational to predict that the issuance of the World Treasury Bank MAiN might well substantially increase, even multiply, the Wall Street valuations of such major Internet sites as noted above, if they are involved, in the online, currency issuance to the convenience and money benefit of their users and fans. *New users sign on forever.*

The download is further described in the First of Twenty-three Currency-Validations by World Treasury Bank. Fun Disruptor Chapter Four.

Herewith a prediction of three additional supporters of the Currency-Validation download:

Forbes' Global 2,000 corporate boards may praise the plan a lot, due to a free, one Billion MAiN distribution to each Board itself. This is seen in Fun Disruptor Chapter Five,

The Second of Twenty-three Currency-Validations by World Treasury Bank.

The world's 1,426 Billionaires may praise the plan a lot. One Billion MAiN currency-validation to *each* of the world's 1,426 billionaires, a doable 1,426 Billion, 1,426,000,000,000 M}. A billionaire can like an additional billion. Whatever. This is seen in Fun Disruptor Chapter Seven, The Fourth of Twenty-three Currency-Validations.

Fully **ten thousand entertainment and sports celebrities** worldwide may enthuse for weeks on television in 100 nations. Due to receiving one million MAiN each as a swag bag. It is good to be famous. This is seen in Fun Disruptor Chapter Six, The Third of Twenty-three Currency-Validations by World Treasury Bank.

Department of Who Would Have Guessed: Congress, and the Democratic National Committee, and the Republican National Committee stand to be, unexpectedly, really pleased. This is seen in Fun Disruptor Chapter Thirteen.

A major, proactive principle and mantra of World Treasury Bank MAiN is that *each vendor worldwide is paid solely in their own, home-currency.* Just as Americans, travelling abroad with a Bank of America credit card, can purchase yuan and euro and yen goods because the currency-exchange is made automatically. That is, MAiN forex is done, by smartphone, on the buyer's savings account, on the World Treasury Bank site.

There is no interest by World Treasury Bank MAiN, there is proactive disinterest, in being any nation's legal tender, ever. World Treasury Bank MAiN is specifically *unwilling* to become legal tender in any nation. Not Wal-Mart nor Domino's Pizza nor Helen's Hair Styling will ever be asked to accept MAiN.

There is now, and forever, no attempt to have the MAiN, a U.S. Legal Tender, nor interest in any such bizarre thing.

The World Treasury Bank MAiN is a smartphone-only, smartphone-everything currency. It is Internet-only. No notes or coins, *ever*.

Just a thought: the late, great Steve Jobs might likely wish that he had created the MAiN in the iPhone. His excellent successors might consider the World Treasury Bank MAiN app.

It is worth noting in passing that reportedly some stores in Sweden have a sign on the door, No Cash Accepted. We usually think of cash as being the mother's milk of retail stores. Yet, cash is expensive to handle. It needs counting. It needs recounting, sometimes by a supervisor. It is subject to loss and pilferage and robbery. It needs a safe. It requires a time consuming daily trip to the bank. It has inconvenient little coins.

World Treasury Bank and MAiN may be able to have Google-like dominance in: Internet banking worldwide. In online currency. In online loans. In Payments, which see in the Profits section herein. Fun Disruptor Chapter Nine.

The Plan may make the first Triple-digit Billionaires. Fun Disruptor Chapter Eight. Department of Who Would Have Guessed: World Treasury Bank MAiN Founders will be *acclaimed as worldwide leaders*, for decades. This is seen, convincingly we like to think, in the Currency-Validations throughout this book. As listed in Contents.

Department of Who Would Have Predicted: most national legislators worldwide may not oppose the existence of the private-sector, universal currency. This is seen in the stunningly attractive Currency-Validations by World Treasury Bank MAiN. Fun Disruptor Chapters Ten through Twenty. Are these each unique and compelling? You be the judge.

World Treasury Bank stands to be able to work successfully with regulators.

The above-noted offers a treasure trove of material for You-Tube and Facebook and Twitter entrants in the opportunity to apply for very large awards that might be paid out. Fun Disruptor Awards Chapter Thirty.

Fun Disruptor Chapter Three
ON DAY ONE, BIGGER THAN ANY OTHER BANK

Four Litmus Tests that Major Players Can Consider

Litmus Test One

That the Plan is for a business that can quickly be bigger than Apple, Inc., a great, great corporation, in (a) Wall Street valuation, and (b) worldwide popular enthusiasm.

Litmus Test Two

Inexpensive to launch. World Treasury Bank distributes money, not needs money. That is, the major players, say, a bunch of billionaires and others, are not needed for much investment. They are desirable and necessary for probity. For business expertise at the highest level.

One area of World Treasury Bank MAiN that is not inexpensive to launch is data centers. The data centers need to be large enough for perhaps *two* savings accounts for each of perhaps 2,000,000,000 to 3,000,000,000 savings accounts. Why two? Because each person can have a World Treasury Bank MAiN account, and, a World Treasury Bank Home-Currency Account.

There is more data storage needed. World Treasury Bank can offer to each of an immense number of sellers and individuals their own World Treasury Bank MAiN Site home-page. Sellers can sell their wares to buyers in their home nation, and to buyers in 150+ nations. A buyer on any continent who is looking for, say, Sweaters-Cashmere, may be able to buy directly from a seller in Australia, who also has a site on, or click-through to his other site, available through World Treasury Bank site's SELLERS PLANET. Smartphone pay for the cashmere sweater from Melbourne by Intrabank MAiNPay. Fun Disruptor Chapter Nine.

So, large data centers, also known as server farms, are needed. Some major online businesses have begun using Amazon Web Services, which has a very high reputation, and rents by the month for space used, rather than a long-term contract for servers, which may turn out not to be needed. (Google, Netflix uses Amazon Web Services). Some firms later conclude that they want their own data centers. Nevertheless, a long-term partnership with Amazon Web Services may work for both Amazon and World Treasury Bank MAiN. Just a thought. Microsoft's Azure Cloud Computing Service also has a high reputation among more than half of Fortune 500 firms.

Litmus Test Three

First 24 Hours: Perhaps 10-figures profit on The First Day Open. Perhaps some billions of dollars profit in the first days. From sales of the World Treasury Bank MAiN download app. This is seen in the Profits Section. Fun Disruptor Chapter Nine. If billions in profits in one day proves to be the case, it might be a business first.

Litmus Test Four

Smartphone only, smartphone everything. No bricks-and-mortar except a headquarters building or campus in, perhaps, Hong Kong or the City of London or Singapore or Dublin or Wellington or Silicon Valley.

Bank analysts may say that the business seems *intrinsically* Exxon Mobil size in valuation, virtually born as: **The Largest Bank on Earth**. Be a Founder. Good idea.

World Treasury Bank may have a larger NYSE corporate valuation than most any corporation, and enjoy worldwide popular admiration. You be the judge.

It is Sort-of-Like, as if Facebook issued a currency to 1,000,000,000 accounts.The Bank can issue *The_ Private-Sector*, World Currency via Smartphones. Preferably with Facebook and Apple iTunes, and others.

Nations, even legislators in 150+ nations, may like the plan. As seen in, That World Treasury Bank may be as Powerful as a Major Nation. Fun Disruptor Chapter Twenty.

The above-noted offers a treasure trove of material for YouTube and Facebook and Twitter entrants in the opportunity to apply for very large awards that might be paid out. Fun Disruptor Awards Chapter Thirty.

Chapter Four
DOWNLOAD A FREE 10,000 MAIN TO EVERY SMARTPHONE. THANKS, BILLIONAIRES

The First of Twenty-three Currency-Validations by World Treasury Bank MAiN that Really Please Humanity.

This is How Billionaires Can Be Acclaimed Worldwide for Decades by Popular, Liberating Actions from World Treasury Bank MAiN, and its Founders.

This First Currency-Validation is based on the 'Helicopter Ben' Bernanke-Milton Friedman thesis that sometimes the best way for the Federal Reserve to allocate dollar distribution would be, in ultimate effect, to 'have helicopters drop money to the people below'. The helicopters are tongue-in-cheek of course. But the thesis is serious about a worthy allocation of currency issuance.

Better, download to smartphones.

The Plan herein is that 2,000,000,000 smartphone users, perhaps 3,000,000,000, in 150+ nations can download the World Treasury Bank MAiN app.

THEN: download 10,000 MAiN each, for Free, to their app-opened, automatic World Treasury Bank MAiN Savings Account. It may be worth noting that even app game makers go live simultaneously, same day, in 125 nations. World Treasury Bank MAiN can go live simultaneously in 196 nations.

Our game is somewhat bigger and better.

The World Treasury Bank download may cause national and world enjoyment for weeks. Seen on nightly TV news. Visibly happy, excited people may line up at cellphone stores, worldwide, to buy smartphones in anticipation.

To spend their MAiN: in the World Treasury Bank MAiN site, recipients FOREX MAiN for their Home-Currency, on their smartphone. Takes ten seconds.

THEN: smartphone-transfer to their Home-Currency Bank Account.

A Home-Currency Savings Account can be a World Treasury Bank account as well: "One-click to CREATE YOUR Home-Currency SAVINGS ACCOUNT".

World Economic Forum, in a report with McKinsey, says that the world needs $100 Trillion in additional capital over the next 10 years. Where is this money going to come from?

We have a suggestion.

Numbers: The Largest 1,000 Banks in the World reportedly have assets in excess of $100 Trillion. This is an average of $50,000 per household on earth, assuming two Billion households on the planet.

Consider that other banks' assets and other liquidity totals another $100 Trillion. This $200 Trillion is roughly three times the World Gross Annual Product of about $75 Trillion.

This $200 Trillion is inconveniently, somewhat ludicrously, spread among more than 90 fiat currencies of uncertain value, though the declining U.S. dollar functions as the reserve currency. Having ninety different currencies is fine, except that *they are a huge brake on world commerce.*

Perhaps 100 Trillion in MAiN, over ten years, may be a necessary issuance for world liquidity.

This might drive World Annual Product to grow at a faster rate.

As suggested in the hypothesis of Switzerland issuing a worldwide, online currency called the 'Zurich', related, if 200 nations and states of the world jointly issued an additional currency, called the Global, **the action would be praised worldwide as a locomotive of prosperity**. They might issue 10 to 12 Trillion 'Globals' a year.

Alas, the unsolvable problem, at least unsolved over the past 2,000 years, perhaps twenty-five percent to fifty percent of the nations would be like Greece and Argentina and Zimbabwe in off-the-books debt, and pressing desire for inflation. These nations would be able to vote for the 'Global Treasury Bank' chairman. This is a scary thought. We suppose that the Zimbabwean guy could at least offer that his nation has a lot of experience in issuing currency. The MAiN is much better.

Advised by currency experts, MAiN issuance, over ten years, would be a To-Be-Determined number, a percentage, perhaps 12% - 15%, of the Gross World Product number, which is $75 trillion a year, $750+ trillion in 10 years, a mind-numbing 1,000 Trillion in less than 15 years.

Twelve per cent of the latter would be: World Treasury Bank issuing: 120 Trillion MAiN, over 10+ years, about one Trillion per month, if issued.

Worth noting, former U.S. Federal Reserve Chairman, Paul A. Volcker, has apparently called for a world currency, "Towards a Single World Currency to Level the Playing Field", New York Times, January 31, 2000.

Yet, as noted herein, we do not believe that an all-nations system can work, due to the historic folly of legislatures. Due to malfeasance. Due to hidden and hostile agendas. Paul Volcker is a very wise man and should be consulted herein.

The MAiN is to Be an Asset that the Central Banks Cannot Print.

It may be asked, if it is a good idea to give the people of a nation 10,000 MAiN for free, then why should not any nation do the same thing with its own currency? The reason would appear to be inflation, which grievously disadvantages savers and shoppers.

Ultimately, there is a tad of murkiness in this whole area. Perhaps if all living Nobel Prize winners in economics gathered together, and collegially discussed the plan herein, at the end of their brilliant review, they would admit to....some murkiness, some admitted unknowns. Human beings cannot do omniscience.

The MAiN is perhaps likely a fiat currency. Yet, MAiN is not hobbled by a 1. National Budget, 2. National debt or 3. Need to tax or 4. 'Need' to inflate.

Each nation is responsible for its own folly, addiction to spending, and debt. The fact that Nation A inflates, has no effect whatever on the Swiss Franc. Each Parliament and Congress is free to stop spending money it does not have and cannot get.

It may be that the MAiN should be tied to gold. Gold is important because of human folly, which is never in short supply.

Another measurement of how much MAiN should be issued by World Treasury Bank may be seen in a Laffer-genre curve. Picture the St. Louis Gateway Arch as a graph. At one ground-side of the Arch, if there is no MAiN issued at all, the value of

MAiN is zero. At the other ground-side of the Arch graph, if there are Zimbabwean hundreds of trillions of MAiN issued, the value again would be zero.

The correct amount of MAiN to be issued may be the amount that gives the highest value for the MAiN, at the apogee of the Arch graph. This amount is not known yet by any mortals. But there are some indices, for example, gold.

A Lot of Joy for Humanity

The download of 10,000 MAiN to perhaps literally billions of smartphone users worldwide may cause a great deal of pleasure to humans in this vale of tears. It may be that television news worldwide will be chock full of heartwarming stories of how 10,000 MAiN, forexed to the recipient's home-currency account, saved a family from being evicted. In Sao Paulo, not evicted. In South Side Chicago, not evicted. In South Africa, not evicted. In Sydney, not evicted. In a posh suburb of New York, not evicted.

Other examples may be of how getting 10,000 MAiN allowed a man and wife to buy a food cart, a little business, which has saved them from being homeless on the street in Buenos Aires, or Nairobi. Now, they and their children are getting by. The kids' faces, smiling up at dad and mom. The kids help out at the food cart. The food cart may have been purchased on World Treasury Bank's Seller's Planet. Fun Disruptor Chapter Nine.

There stand to be a lot of tearful expressions of gratitude from people in many nations. And high fiving by persons given an unexpected, advantageous gift that helps them out in life's struggles.

The Billionaires Helped Us

Some people remark happily, on five continents, "The billion aires helped us." This is, How Billionaires Become Popular.

There are other ways in later chapters that come under the heading, How Billionaires Became Popular.

This is kind of a new thing.

The above-noted offers a treasure trove of material for YouTube and Facebook and Twitter entrants in the opportunity to apply for very large awards that might be paid out. Fun Disruptor Awards Chapter Thirty.

Fun Disruptor Chapter Five
A BILLION MAIN TO EACH
OF 2,000 LARGEST
CORPORATION BOARDS

The Second of Twenty-three Currency-Validations by World Treasury Bank MAiN that Please Humanity. Or at least many VIPs.

This is How Billionaires Can Be Acclaimed Worldwide for Decades by Popular, Liberating Actions from World Treasury Bank, the MAiN, and its Founders.

The Plan includes a notably striking Currency-Validation distribution, perhaps world-stunning. You be the judge:

One Billion MAiN to *each* of the **Boards of Directors-themselves of Forbes' Global 2,000 Largest Corporations**.
Including U.S. Major Media and other Big Media.
And including the board members of the 100 or 1,000 largest labor unions.

Say, 100,000,000 MAiN to *each* Board Member.

Each interested Board would file with the S.E.C., or the equivalent in other nations, a Board Resolution to accept the One Billion MAiN Currency-Validation distribution.

This would create 20,000 Board Member fans in the 2,000 largest corporations worldwide, and in labor unions.

Worldwide, people would be thinking, "Wow!"

Consider that each of 20,000 board members of the 2,000 largest corporations and labor unions in the world personally knows 1,000 business people and friends and club members and employees and former employees and acquaintances and members. This is 20,000,000 people.

Perhaps they each virally spread the word to many others. This may make excellent *Currency-Validation by people worldwide noting that the corporate and finance and union VIPs own MAiN.*

Some observers, perhaps from one part of the political spectrum, might comment, "Why give large money to the wealthy?" Though not all board members are wealthy. But some are.

Here is the reason: There are *Only Three Things* that the rich person can do with his or her wealth.

First of Three Things

The rich person can invest his or her wealth, in their own business, or in equities, buying on the stock market. Perhaps invest in start-ups. This investing helps the economy. It helps poor people.

Second of Three Things

The rich person can put part of their wealth in thought-to-be safe places such as treasuries, money market accounts, municipal bonds that are not in California or Illinois, and so on. This investing helps the economy. It helps poor people. The money helps the young couple in Dubuque or Dalian or Durban get their first home mortgage. It helps the small business person get a loan to expand his or her business.

Third of Three Things

The actual rich (not just upper-middle class people called 'rich') can live the high-end life: multiple expensive homes, expensive cars, high-end travel, expensive apparel, high-end restaurants, maybe a yacht, support charities, and so on. This spending helps the economy. It helps poor people. Millions of people in the U.S. and abroad make a good living in the luxury trade, and raise their families and send their kids to college by doing so.

In summation, the answer to the question, What will Board Members do with their perhaps 100,000,000 MAiN each?, is:

They can convert MAiN to their home-currency or other currencies.

They can keep part of their MAiN in World Treasury Bank, waiting for the exchange rate to solidify.

They can invest it. They can spend it. It all helps the economy.

The above-noted offers a treasure trove of material for You-Tube and Facebook and Twitter entrants in the opportunity to apply for very large awards that might be paid out. Fun Disruptor Awards Chapter Thirty.

Fun Disruptor Chapter Six
1,000,000 MAIN TO EACH OF
10,000 CELEBRITIES

The Third of Twenty-three Currency-Validations by World Treasury Bank MAiN that Humanity Can Enjoy

This is How Billionaires Can Be Acclaimed Worldwide for Decades by Popular, Liberating Actions from World Treasury Bank, the MAiN, and its Founders.

Happy Celebrities Worldwide

A Currency-Validation Distribution of: 1,000,000 MAiN to *each* of **10,000 to 15,000 celebrities**, perhaps more. These would be motion picture, television, music and sports celebrities worldwide.

Most every nation has major celebrities, sometimes much loved heroes of stage or sports field, who are unknown to any other nation.

World Treasury Bank MAiN can list the, say, 100 major celebrities of each of 150 nations. Perhaps 15,000 celebs. The list may be able to be built by Google search of each nation. Biggest music stars in, say, the Philippines. Biggest singing stars in the Philippines. Biggest movie stars in the Philippines. Biggest sports stars in the Philippines.

And so on for each nation. Movie and Television and Music and Sports celebrities, worldwide. NO, we will certainly *not* exclude Reese Witherspoon! RW has turned away from her life of crime, and we love her. Hello!

Perhaps, 10,000, or more, Commentators and Columnists get the 1,000,000 MAiN: "Full disclosure, I have chosen to accept...." This is something that needs to be examined. At least, nothing under the table, of course. People may admire that Commentators and Columnists and Editors take advantage of the Currency-Validation gift. "To my readers: I have five children to send to college. Therefore, with my Editor's permission, I have decided to accept the one million MAiN distribution. I do not believe that I have lost my critical judgment. You, my readers, can judge."

The 1,000,000 MAiN to each celebrity makes an extraordinary 'swag bag', perhaps reported worldwide, and talked about enthusiastically on entertainment TV and sports television, in 150 nations, for days. Or weeks: It would be particularly notable if the value of the free market MAiN proves to be, lo and behold, worth, say, the U.S. dollar out the door.

If nothing of this value arises, celebrities and others can "wait until the value appreciates."

Entertainment and sports celebrities may be discussing the World Treasury Bank MAiN Currency-Validation event in pleased, delighted, and other upbeat terms for weeks on television interviews, and tweets, in 150+ nations.

The above-noted offers a treasure trove of material for YouTube and Facebook and Twitter entrants in the opportunity to apply for very large awards that might be paid out. Fun Disruptor Awards Chapter Thirty

Fun Disruptor Chapter Seven
A BILLION MAIN TO EACH OF THE WORLD'S BILLIONAIRES

The Fourth of Twenty-three Currency-Validations by World Treasury Bank MAiN that Actually Pleases Humanity.

To Please the World's Billionaires

World Treasury Bank can, in Currency-Validation, give to *each* of the world's 1,426 <u>billionaires</u>, 1,000,000,000 MAiN. This is a doable 1,426 Billion, M} 1,426,000,000,000. This would tend to be world stunning.

People will say, "Wow!"
This might allow a billionaires association worldwide, if this is a good idea.

The investments by major wealth people will help many, many millions of people. And further validate the MAiN.

Some commentators will of course say, Why give this huge amount of money to already very wealthy individuals? Why not give it to the poor? The World Treasury Bank MAiN response is that the First of Twenty-three Currency-Validations by World

Treasury Bank MAiN that Really Please Humanity does precisely that, 10,000 MAiN to each of 2,000,000,000 smartphone owners. Perhaps 3,000,000,000. That is 30 Trillion MAiN. That is, 30,000,000,000,000. Thirteen zeroes. *It is a Major Historic Event of the sort that is written in history books in a century or two.* No pouting!

Secondly, the investments by the billionaires will create innumerable jobs, and money in banks for home mortgages, and so on.

Thirdly, the fact that major wealth men and women hold the MAiN may well increase the value of the MAiN unto itself. This helps everyone in the world who has a smartphone. Some billionaires may say that they are leaving their MAiN in "my savings account at World Treasury Bank." This may increase the value of the MAiN.

Joe Smith is greatly pleased to be banking at the same bank as 1,426 Billionaires. Joe has been boasting non-stop about, "banking where the Billionaires bank." Joe is a Thousandaire.

The Money Summit, say in Beijing, or wherever it is held, can be held annually if desired. Just a thought: perhaps the Money Summit could be held with the World Economic Forum, of Davos, which convenes an annual meeting in Dalian, China.

Bitcoin and Company

Randall E. Forsyth, in the always superb Barron's, April 13, 2013, "The rush to the Bitcoin may have been a speculative bubble, but it may also represent *an inchoate search for an alternative to government-controlled paper currencies...* [Italics added].

"Someday, an alternative to gold that doesn't require the tedious and expensive mining, storage, and transfer of the metal may be conjured. Those difficulties gave rise to paper money, which is being abused. For now, gold no longer is loved, which, to an independent-minded contrarian investor, only adds to its allure."

We propose World Treasury Bank's MAiN.

Quoting from The Economist, as quoted by Henry Blodget in his great and necessary daily online read for business people, Business Insider, April 14, 2013, "A less nerdy alternative is Ripple. It will be much easier to use than Bitcoin, says Chris Larsen, a serial entrepreneur from Silicon Valley and co-founder of OpenCoin, the start-up behind Ripple. Transactions are approved (or not) in a few seconds, compared with the ten minutes a typical Bitcoin trade takes to be confirmed. There is no mystery about the origins of Ripple nor (yet) any association with criminal or other dubious activities.

"OpenCoin is expected to start handing out Ripples to the public in May. It has created 100 billion, a number it promises never to increase. To give the new currency momentum, Open-Coin plans eventually to give away 75% of the supply. Anyone opening an OpenCoin account will receive five Ripples; existing Bitcoin users will get more.

"The 25% retained by OpenCoin will give it a huge incentive to make sure that the Ripple is strong: the higher its value, the bigger the reward for OpenCoin's investors when the firm cashes out. On April 10th several blue-chip venture-capital firms, including the ultra-hip Andreessen Horowitz, announced that they had invested in OpenCoin.

"If Ripple gains traction, even bigger financial players may enter the fray. A firm such as Visa could create its own cheap instant international-payments system, notes BitPay's Mr. Gallippi. And what if a country were to issue algorithmic money?"

We greatly admire the players here. They are absolutely first-rate people. Andreessen Horowitz, great, great. We should meet.

Yet, we respectfully ask, which is unmistakably the best plan? We respectfully point out that the above-noted 100 billion is only 14 Ripples for each human being on the planet. Even street urchins in Lagos may wrinkle their noses. And Ripple, a two syllable, word has no meaning and is frivolous to stressed-out people-and-their-money.

The above could be wrong.

Is it?

The above-noted offers a treasure trove of material for YouTube and Facebook and Twitter entrants in the opportunity to apply for very large awards that might be paid out. Fun Disruptor Awards Chapter Thirty.

Fun Disruptor Chapter Eight
THE MAKING OF TRIPLE-DIGIT BILLIONAIRES, POPULAR WORLDWIDE

Say just for speculative example, 100 Trillion MAiN comes to be loaned out at a minimal 3% worldwide. This would be Three Trillion profit a year.

If World Treasury Bank MAiN is valued at only 10 times earnings, this would be a Thirty Trillion valuation of the Bank. 13 zeroes. 30,000,000,000,000. It is as if 200 nations and states issued the MAiN. This plan is much better.

One percent ownership of Thirty Trillion is a Seems-Too-High-to-be-Correct-Arithmetic 300 Billion. 300,000,000,000. It is 11 zeroes. Count, uh, *Your* zeroes.
Double these numbers for six percent.

MAiN might become worth the dollar. This means that there may be a number of First Mover investor individuals and corporations that **become worth Three Hundred Billion Dollars** in World Treasury Bank MAiN stock.

Unexpectedly, the corporations and individual Founders of World Treasury Bank will be *acclaimed as worldwide leaders*. They will be acclaimed for decades as seen throughout this book. For example, the 10,000 free MAiN given to 2,000,000,000 to 3,000,000,000 smartphone owners who download 10,000 MAiN into their World Treasury Bank MAiN Savings Account.

Additional reasons that World Treasury Bank MAiN Founders become actual heroes to humanity are each seen in Contents. They include:

World Treasury Bank MAiN University, The Bank will obtain the annual endowment for free, streaming university for all human beings forever. This is, a major, enduring advance for the world. Plus, streaming K-12 grade school, at top world class level, in 10 major languages. Free forever. Fun Disruptor Chapter Ten.

The World Parliament of Women. A World Treasury Bank app will allow 3,000,000,000 women to vote online for 500 women representatives to the *world-shaping* Parliament. With dozens of streaming TV channels from the Parliament. Men, be afraid, be very afraid. Fun Disruptor Chapter Eleven.

The Emancipation Proclamation for All Women Worldwide. Fun Disruptor Chapter Twelve.

Congress TV Channel. A 15-minute, *Show and Say Anything from Anywhere* segment, every two weeks, for each member of Congress, A-Z. This means that World Treasury Bank MAiN has 535 Best Friends Forever in Congress. What is wrong with people loving each other? Hello! Love is power. It is good to be powerful. Fun Disruptor Chapter Thirteen.

Democratic Party TV Channel, and, Republican Party TV Channel, in side-by-side studio buildings in D.C.

Side-by-side at their request, due to love. 535 Even Better than Best Friends Forever. It is good to have even more power. Fun Disruptor Chapter Thirteen.

Grade School at Top World Class Level for All Americans. Fun Disruptor Chapters Seventeen, Eighteen.

Rich Corporations Can Become The Richest Ever 1

The fore-noted Substantial Historic Advancements constitute some of a number of reasons that major world Internet sites can be and we suggest *should be* a part of World Treasury Bank, and as Founders. The most important sites such as **Y**ahoo, **G**oogle, **F**acebook, Apple **i**Tunes, LinkedIn, **B**aidu, **M**snbc.com, **T**encent, **T**witter, **S**ina Weibo, **A**libaba. Your own logos with click-through to your home-page can be on the World Treasury Bank MAiN home-page, and perhaps on every one of 2,000,000,000, to-be 3,000,000,000, World Treasury Bank Account Holders' pages.

Consider a 10% Bonus in the Free Download of 10,000 World Treasury Bank MAiN for: persons who use their major site-name email as part of their ID. **The world crowds onto the involved sites, signing up forever**. Unlike romantic love, love of money endures.

Maybe-could-be, the same bonus to Private Equity Clients, and Unit Holders, and Individual Investors.

Rich Corporations Can Become The Richest Ever 2

There can be another bonus: **10% of gross MAiN issuance to go to** Yahoo, and Apple, et al, the above-noted site corporations. This would be *Huge, Historic Profit*. Ten percent of 30 Trillion is 3,000 Billion. Three Trillion. This is quite a large sum. Twelve zeroes, 3,000,000,000,000.

Wall Street *may multiply the valuation* of such as the above-noted major Internet sites and corporations if they are involved.

Let's meet and kick this around. How about lunch at Madera, on the Terrace? You pay. ...Okay, okay, Dutch.

As the de facto Business Plan involves World Treasury Bank MAiN major players, investments may be made over perhaps 12 months, with opportunity to suspend or stop.

This is the Media Era

At Critical Mass of major players, the Founders Group may as well invite each of *the largest five U.S. media corporations* to be participants. Each can always disclose in their news reports, 'Name of Media' holds stock in World Treasury Bank MAiN.

Each and all of the five major U.S. media corporations should in logic participate. The reasons are two: Immense profits beyond any that can be made elsewhere. Above.

And: the advancements for all humanity, above-noted, and as listed in the Contents of this book.

For Your Review

World Treasury Bank will have *Zero Cost of Money*.

The Bank can variously loan a lot of money worldwide.

Unlimited Capital: World Treasury Bank MAiN has, sort of at least, Unlimited Capital.

What does this mean?

The Largest IPO Ever May Be Possible: Chapter Nine.

Earlier we referred to Nobel Prize recipients in Economics, if all gathered together, to review the plan, would still leave some murkiness, some Known Unknowns in their review. That is the case here. As noted above, a lot of advancement for humanity, serious historic stuff, actual liberation, can be done by World

Treasury Bank MAiN (paid for by 10,000+ foundations in annual convention). World Treasury Bank Founders get credit and a truly historic legacy.

What do you think?

The makers of the personal computer, Bill Gates and company, are said not to have seen that Word Processing would be huge, and would do to the typewriter business what the automobile did to the horse-and-buggy. The point here is that the future, even future advantages, cannot be known even by The Makers of the Future.

The above-noted offers a treasure trove of material for You-Tube and Facebook and Twitter entrants in the opportunity to apply for very large awards that might be paid out. Fun Disruptor Awards Chapter Thirty.

Fun Disruptor Chapter Nine
POTENTIAL PROFIT

Day 1 Profit – Potentially 10-figures

If the World Treasury Bank, MAiN download-APP itself, to 2,000,000,000 smartphones, cost the downloader only $2.00 to $4.00, to get 10,000 MAiN for free, this may prove to be a *$4,000,000,000 to $8 Billion dollars profit*, on Day 1. This is speculation of course, yet may be worth consideration.

The 2,000,000,000 stands to become 3,000,000,000. China Mobile alone has 740,000,000 subscribers.

If the charge for the World Treasury Bank App was only $4.00, this could be conceivably perhaps $8,000,000,000 to twelve billion dollars *profit* in the first few days or weeks.

If not offered for free: the price for the Download-10,000-MAiN app might be: Month 1 - $2.00 Month 2: $4.00 Month 3: $6.00 Month 4: $8.00 Month 5: $10.00, equaling potentially, just to speculate, $10 to $20 Billion in profit, a huge profit virtually at no cost. This may draw investment banks for a major, talk-of-the-world Initial Public Offering.

MAiNPay Payments Center among 2 Billion to 3,000,000,000 Buyers and Sellers Worldwide

Compare Facebook's 1,000,000,000 accounts (we are huge, huge admirers of Mark Zuckerberg and we should meet) to what-may-be 2,000,000,000 to 3,000,000,000 World Treasury Bank Savings Account holders.

This intrinsically creates a giant Payment System, <u>MAiN-Pay</u>, a financial eco-system, among 2,000,000,000+ people and businesses worldwide.

To pay a bill: pay by Smartphone on WTB *INTRABANK* MAiN-Pay. Pay to the payee's MAiNPay Email: _____@ MAiNPay.com. This may supersede other banks, wires, checks, and bank cards. PayPal, Square, Wallet may integrate with World Treasury Bank MAiNPay, their click-through logos everywhere, perhaps located on each one of 2-3,000,000,000 pages. Moreover, each World Treasury Bank account holder is to have two WTB saving accounts. One savings account in MAiN. A second savings account in his or her home-currency.

100,000,000 smartphone intrabank payments a day worldwide at <u>30 cents each</u> would be $30 million dollars a *day* profit times 365 would be $11 Billion a year profit.

200,000,000 smartphone intrabank payments a day worldwide at <u>30 cents each</u> would be $60 million dollars a *day* profit times 365 would be $22 Billion a year profit.

Instead of Employee Costs, a Profit Center

International trade is variously calculated to be about $25 trillion a year. There may be room here, with growth, for substantial World Treasury Bank MAiN trade loans. We will find out.

A World Treasury Bank loan officer, worldwide, is: An experienced banker with an ultrabook, and Skype. No bricks-and-mortar at all. He or she is paid solely in commissions from loan repayments. They purchase the franchise called, **World Treasury Bank, Vice President, Loan Officer**. They meet daily at 'Starbucks' as a local, loan review committee.

For example, 100,000 banker-franchisees, for 100 nations, an average of 1,000 per nation, loaning out 10,000,000 a month each, equals One Trillion a month. No pay for lending, ever. They might loan solely to businesses that own or will buy their own land and buildings, like McDonald's. Rock solid. They loan only in the home-currency, except as MAiN is allowed.

Money can be loaned to banks, as allowed.

Money might be loaned online, worldwide.

World Treasury Bank may purchase a small Internet-only U.S. bank that is chartered in all 50 states.

World Treasury Bank MAiN may require all of its bankers to be able to speak English, for daily, worldwide, online sharing of information on the World Treasury Bank site. English is the world language for business in any case.

Profit from Advertising

A click-through on each of 2,000,000,000 to 3,000,000,000 World Treasury Bank pages, may be titled:

'See Ads'

Clicking down can give a drop-down menu such as: Automobiles. Apparel. Electronics. Travel. Random. Etcetera. And: "Suggest ads YOU would like to see."

And: Turn-off Ads

SELLERS PLANET

World Treasury Bank MAiN plans to have a search section, Sellers Planet. This is currently planned as a free listing of click-through to sellers' web sites. Such as Amazon.com. There could be nine or ten figures in listed sellers. Listed by Product. Listed by Language. Listed by Nation. Google and eBay and Chinese and Indian and other selling sites could have, on Sellers Planet home-pages, full-page click-through to their sites.

Increased World Prosperity

Individuals and businesses, sellers and buyers of goods and services worldwide, may use the universality of MAiN for customer convenience, and *INTRABANK*, instant payment system. <u>To multiply international sales</u>: Online sellers may quote prices in MAiN as well as their home-currency. MAiN, <u>The</u> World Exchange. This may <u>disintermediate</u> a world of Warehouses-Distributors-Wholesalers-Retailers.

Twenty-five per cent of all the goods and services produced in all history have been produced in the past 10 years. The MAiN may add to such economic growth, and a large, rapid expansion of world trade, and new prosperity, for billions of people.

Worth noting: There is 5 Trillion dollars volume a day, <u>$1,825 Trillion a year</u>, almost two quadrillion dollars, in foreign exchange markets. – Bloomberg, March 3, 2012.

As noted earlier, the largest 1,000 banks in the world have assets in excess of $100 Trillion. This is an average of $50,000 per household on earth, assuming two Billion households on the planet.

Consider that other banks' assets and other liquidity totals another $100 Trillion. $200 Trillion is three times the World Gross Annual Product.

What is Your View: How Much MAiN Should Be Issued?

Some Speculative Numbers for Issuance

The World Gross Product is $75 Trillion a year. – CIA World Factbook

Multiplied by 10 years, this is $750 Trillion dollars. Multiplied by 15 years this is over One Quadrillion dollars Gross World Product. A Quadrillion dollars is 1,000 Trillion dollars. You knew that.

Based on this number, it might make sense to issue, over 10 years, 120 months, 100+ Trillion MAiN. Equaling $100 Trillion Dollars if worth dollars. These numbers are preliminary and speculative, and await review by a collegial group of currency experts. The World Treasury Bank MAiN plan of course calls for obtaining continuing independent reviews of the plan.

World Treasury Bank may have 100 Trillion in assets on Day 1. Compare this to what Apple had on Day One. Steve Jobs.

Global household wealth now stands at $235 trillion dollars. – Wall Street Journal, October 14, 2012.

China's banking assets grew by $14 trillion between 2008 and 2013. – Fitch Ratings.

Therefore, the *Seemingly-Too-Large Issuance*, over 10+ years of perhaps 100 Trillion MAiN, electronically, all zeroes-and-ones only.

What is Your View: How Much MAiN Should Be Issued? If you like, pencil-in your number. Shape the world here:

Earlier, in The Making of Triple-digit Billionaires, Popular Worldwide, it was speculated that only one percent ownership of World Treasury Bank might become worth a Seems-Too-High-to-be-Correct-Arithmetic, 300 Billion. Dollars if worth dollars. Fun Disruptor Chapter Eight.

If 200 Nations and States Issued an Additional Online Currency

If 200 nations and states issued an additional, online-only currency, each nation might own less than one percent of World Treasury Bank. It may be that no one party should own a significant percentage of World Treasury Bank MAiN. It may be that if one corporation or individual major player owned more than a small percentage, this would be a public relations disadvantage. And a disadvantage for the growth of the Bank. Perhaps the public, worldwide, would not have the same high regard for the probity of the stock holder that some other people might. Who knows, one percent might prove to be more than five percent.

Three-hundred Billion in personal wealth, may be worth dollars, is quite a bit in any case, when you think about it.

For Worldwide Liquidity for People in 150 Nations

As noted, World Treasury Bank may (or may not) issue 10% or more of the Gross World Product-numbers over 10-12 years of near $1,000 Trillion, that is, perhaps issue 100 Trillion MAiN over 10 years.

There is a currency commentator who compares issuing a World Currency merely to starting up a PayPal-II with a currency.

To Advance the World Treasury Bank Plan Inexpensively:

Early major player participants can bring in a financial executive, nationally-known in the financial world, to convey the Plan to other major players, in the U.S. and abroad. To achieve *Critical Mass* of major participants.

What might attract a nationally-known financial executive to a perhaps interim gig? The potentiality of perhaps a *billion in stock and stock options*. Who should it be?

Steps to Prove the Validity of the Plan

Commission independent reviews of the plan by currency experts.

Decide, when convenient, how many Major Players shall be called 'Critical Mass'. Twenty-five? Whatever.

Decide to bring in a nationally known finance executive to bring in a number of other Major Players.

Get a draft of the whole Money Summit meeting plan, from an event planner in Beijing, or elsewhere. A reference point can be The World Economic Forum at Davos, and at Dalian

Have The Money Summit and World Treasury Bank MAiN websites being created for critical review.

Get the World Treasury Bank download apps for smart-phones and tablets being created. And the World Treasury Bank MAiN back-office software.

The app is also for: World Treasury Bank-foreign exchange (MAiN) transfer to the downloaders Bank in his or her Home-currency (dollars, yuan, Euros, etc.).

That is: to transfer MAiN in his World Treasury Bank Savings Account to his other bank account, the person first clicks "Get foreign-exchange rate: Make exchange." Then clicks, "Transfer (for example) 1,000 MAiN in U.S. dollars to my [as allowed] Bank of America or to my World Treasury Bank-U.S. dollar Savings Account."

The apps are also to include the important, World Treasury Bank MAiN, The World Parliament of Women app, and, The Emancipation Proclamation for All Women Worldwide app. This may create *3,000,000,000, cannot-be-outflanked loyalist fans* of World Treasury Bank MAiN. Fun Disruptor Chapters Eleven and Twelve.

Have a Money Summit central office for Major Players.

Any Participant Can Say on such as CNBC-worldwide Business Channel a Refrain Such as:

"The World Treasury Bank new, private-sector, world currency, the MAiN, *helps middle class and poor people worldwide* because it offers protection against coming inflation.

"Inflation is theft by governments from middle class and poor citizens. Twenty Trillion dollars has been embezzled from middle class and poor Americans, the same in Europe. The middle class is being gutted. *I am very proud to be a part of bringing an inflation-free, universal currency to Seven Billion People on the planet.* People worldwide can make more money and hedge against government theft-by-inflation. Families can be more prosperous."

The Plan may well create the Most Admired Business Leaders on Every Continent in 150 Nations

The Plan is that 2,000,000,000 smartphone users, perhaps 3,000,000,000 in time, in 150+ nations can download the World Treasury Bank app, then *download into their automatic online World Treasury Bank savings account, 10,000 MAiN each, for FREE,* 20 Trillion. Or 30 Trillion. As noted, this stands to be a national and world popular sensation.

Major Player business people and firms from five continents should be able quickly to be successfully invited to participate. These are such as seen in Forbes' list of the world's wealthiest individuals.

Major Players would enjoy being perhaps among, "The Most Admired Men and Women on Earth."

Most admired: Because of World Treasury Bank MAiN University, Free Streaming University for All Human Beings Forever. Because of the World Parliament of Women. Both create long-long term loyalists to World Treasury Bank MAiN.

The Plan assumes that there may well be overreaching attempts to control by regulations. The Plan features a panoply of truly, *actually, world-pleasing responses.* You be the judge whether they are world-pleasing, whether people and powers will talk of them with pleasure in 150 nations. Fun Disruptor Chapters Thirteen, Sixteen, Seventeen, Eighteen, Twenty, Twenty-four, Twenty-seven.

Disruptors Sometimes Can Be Successful Worldwide

Amazon.com *reconceived* the book business. Worldwide.

McDonald's *reconceived* the hamburger business. Worldwide.

Starbucks *reconceived* the coffee shop business. Worldwide.

Costco and Wal-Mart *reconceived* retail shopping. Worldwide.

Apple *reconceived* the cellphone into the smartphone. Worldwide.

iTunes *reconceived* the music business. Worldwide.

The Money Summit, in Beijing or wherever, and World Treasury Bank and the issuance of the MAiN *reconceives* world currency. Worldwide. The world's people will love it.

World Treasury Bank Charter

World Treasury Bank funds are not to be used to pay or to "loan", that is, a "loan" never intended to be repaid, or in any way directly or indirectly to be encumbered by national debts, or the debts or folly of any nation. For this would be to deny to many millions of people around the world a mortgage loan to buy a home, and to deny loans to small business people.

If a nation's credit is strong, it can borrow from its own citizens.

World Treasury Bank Charter

To enjoy a positive reputation worldwide, 5% of the equity of World Treasury Bank will be put directly, irrevocably, into 250 World Treasury Bank MAiN Perpetual Trusts. All of the trusts will be directly or indirectly connected to the causes-world-enjoyment and liberation, **Real Egalitarianism**. Fun Disruptor Chapters Sixteen, Seventeen, Eighteen. (These chapters are about offering the *incredible excitement* of... Mandatory School Homework Schools to all parents. WOW!)

The Plan May Qualify for 'Firstest with the Mostest'

As noted, World Economic Forum/Davos and McKinsey & Company, say that the world needs $100 Trillion dollars in additional liquidity during the next 10 years.

The issuance of 100 Trillion in MAiN might tend to outflank any competing private-sector currency. It would tend to discourage "Us Too" responses. The plan herein for World Treasury Bank invites the main Internet sites to be major-profit involved, and to have their click-through icon on the World Treasury Bank MAiN site, and on each of 2-Billion to 3,000,000,000 bank account pages. And to be on the World Treasury Bank MAiN, Board of Directors. The major Internet sites should be BFF with World Treasury Bank MAiN.

Three Billion Loyalists:

That is, the issuance of the MAiN is not a mere experiment that, if successful, can be expanded. Rather, the issuance of the MAiN is *the real thing unto itself*: the first issuance worldwide of a true world currency.

The World Parliament of Women alone gives World Treasury Bank MAiN three billion Will-Not-Be-Swerved, women Loyalists. Fun Disruptor Chapter Eleven.

World Treasury Bank MAiN says, Welcome to make actual, serious history with us, and *achieve a much greater Wall Street valuation.* Come aboard.

The Largest IPO Ever May Be Possible

The Plan might allow the largest Initial Public Offering ever for World Treasury Bank MAiN. Here is some Sunny Blue Sky speculation, perhaps $100 Billion, four times the size of the largest IPO to date, for a bank in China. The Alibaba IPO may go out with a $105 Billion valuation.-Bloomberg Businessweek, August 26, 2013. This might indicate that World Treasury Bank MAiN pre-IPO valuation may be high-double-digit, or more, billions. The Bank might become worth one or more trillions of dollars. This may allow unique pre-IPO costs for each percentage of the Bank.

There have been recent simultaneous, two-nation IPOs in two different currencies, the Chinese Yuan, and the Singapore dollar. It may well be that the World Treasury Bank MAiN IPO can be a two or more nations IPO, in two or more currencies. Perhaps U.S. dollar, Euro, Yuan, Singapore dollar.

What Do You Think?

Is World Treasury Bank MAiN perhaps **the Next Big Thing** ? Might it be called, 'the Super Big Thing'?

Is the magnitude of The Money Summit, wherever it is held, and World Treasury Bank MAiN, perhaps like more than one Facebook? We are huge admirers of Facebook, and its founder and chief executive. Mark Zuckerberg, when in his twenties, nonchalantly turned down a firm $15.5 billion dollar offer from Microsoft.

That has got to be a first in history.

Is World Treasury Bank as described, perhaps potentially larger than Apple, a great, great corporation, in 1. Wall Street valuation, and 2. worldwide popular enthusiasm? Or not.

Is this a Plan for perhaps, The Largest Business Achievement ever? Might it be called, 'the Great Game'?

What do you think?

What to Do with an Online Bank Network of Two to Three Billion Smartphone Owners

The Plan is that World Treasury Bank will issue 10,000 MAiN, or more, to each of up to 3,000,000,000 smartphone owners. Former Facebook president Sean Parker would, we believe, call these 2,000,000,000 or 3,000,000,000 smartphone owners with a World Treasury Bank MAiN savings account, a "network".

Much might be done with such a network.

MAiNPay and ads are suggested herein.

Perhaps, aggregating business news. Have news feeds by nation and continent and worldwide. Perhaps a human resources site, or integration with a current one that is a first-rate Internet site.

Huge Data, the idea that advanced marketing lies in deep, complex data analytics, not just the power to deliver a lot of eyeballs.

Perhaps a worldwide daily online news 'paper', with innumerable sub-editions for every town. Its name, The MAiN Daily. Cover the White House. Yet, also cover high school girls volleyball playoffs in a rural town in Argentina.

Headquarters and Corporate Domicile of World Treasury Bank

The Plan calls for the Corporate Domicile of World Treasury Bank to be in a tax-free locale, perhaps a negotiated tax-free arrangement in, just for examples, Singapore, New Zealand, Tel Aviv, Dublin, Luxembourg, Cook Islands, Cayman Islands, British Virgin Islands. IF desirable, the MAiN may be issued interim as, technically, a government currency, by a Caribbean Island nation.

The headquarters buildings of World Treasury Bank MAiN may be in any of the above or Hong Kong or Singapore or to-be-decided. In due course, the Plan calls for World Treasury Bank to be headquartered in the U.S., perhaps in Miami for tax reasons. Or will New York show us sincere love?

Potential line of credit, if desired

Facebook secured a $2.5 Billion line of credit, later doubled to $5 Billion shortly before the IPO, arranged by five banks, led by J.P. Morgan Chase.

World Treasury Bank may well be able to secure a, say, **$5 to $10 Billion credit line**.

A major purpose: To acquire **data banks/server farms**, as Apple and Google and Facebook have on various continents. Data space for two accounts for each of 2,000,000,000, maybe 3,000,000,000 World Treasury Bank MAiN Savings Accounts worldwide. Perhaps acquire data banks with Amazon Web Services.

Additionally, among 2,000,000,000 to 3,000,000,000 individuals and businesses big and small, and with MAiNPay, and MAiNMessage, and SELLERS PLANET, a great number of World Treasury Bank Account Holders may find it useful to have a page or a site about themselves or their business, or both, in the World Treasury Bank site. Sellers Planet can also offer, "One-Click to Create Your Site."

World Treasury Bank MAiN site may have free MAiNCall and MAiNChat features worldwide.

All of the above require large data centers.

The World Treasury Bank MAiN Plan may create the richest individuals and Internet corporations in the world.

The above-noted offers a treasure trove of material for You-Tube and Facebook and Twitter entrants in the opportunity to apply for very large awards that might be paid out. Fun Disruptor Awards Chapter Thirty.

Fun Disruptor Chapter Ten
FREE, STREAMING, UNIVERSITY,FOR ALL HUMAN BEINGS, FOREVER

The Fifth of Twenty-three Currency-Validations by World Treasury Bank MAiN that Really Please Humanity.

This is How Billionaires Can Be Acclaimed Worldwide for Decades by Popular, Liberating Actions from World Treasury Bank, the MAiN, and its Founders.

World Acclaim for World Treasury Bank Founders, for Decades

World Treasury Bank MAiN will arrange, perhaps along with major media, the "1,000" foundations, actually "10,000" foundations and 10,000 to 100,000 wealthy persons, Annual-Endowment-Convention, in Las Vegas, for: the *free, streaming university, with every course under the sun.* Undergrad to Ph.D. in everything.

The name of the university is, World Treasury Bank MAiN University. MAiN U, to be loved in 200 nations and states. Streaming from Southern California or Florida.

World Treasury Bank MAiN University is to build, try to forgive this, a large, beautiful, physical campus, with physically attending students. Some people would ask, Why bother having a rolling greens, beautiful buildings, physical campus for an Internet streaming university? We think that students worldwide will greatly enjoy the virtual experience of a university home-page that is: Panning cameras views of the university with the physically-attending students seen going to and from lectures, chatting in the restaurants and so on.

The plan, try to forgive this, is to have men's and women's sports teams in the major world sports, including basketball, football/soccer, cricket whatever that is, American college football, and so on. This could lead to literally one billion students and alumni of World Treasury Bank MAiN University having the common denominator of 'the Big Game'.

Foreign students studying currently at U.S. universities love the whole rah rah, shout-your-lungs-out atmosphere of the Big Game on Friday night or Saturday afternoon. Most universities worldwide are redbrick grim.

As it takes time to build all of the buildings of a major campus, the plan herein is to build temporary, semi-permanent structures of the type that take thirty days to put up. Every lecture and lab can occur in these structures. Though such buildings do have heating and air conditioning, advantage can be taken of a Sun Belt climate in Florida or California.

Meanwhile, the very beautiful permanent buildings, and rolling lawns, and gardens, great clock tower, permanent campus can be being built at top speed next door. The growth of the glorious campus of World Treasury Bank MAiN University can be streamed to the world for hours every day.

World Treasury Bank MAiN University can begin with all of the 'STEM' subjects, science, technology, engineering and math. Then, expand systematically to 'every course under the sun'. Including, Sixteenth Century Bulgarian Poetry. Really. A streaming DVD course. Engineering will include every type of engineering (except how to build the bomb), including space, aeronautical and naval engineering.

A Signature of Every Lecture and Lab at World Treasury Bank MAiN U

Each and every lecture room and lab at World Treasury Bank MAiN University will have, for worldwide proactivity, "10" big screens and "10" video cameras.

Each and every lecture at MAiN University is to take questions and comments from *five continents*, and from each nation that has over one billion population, China and India.

Computers can immediately grade most tests at MAiN University, in a minute. This allows the student to re-do and improve the test on the spot, or the next day. Cheating!

The lectures will be in English. Yet, DVDs may be captioned in any language. For example, a man or woman in India wants to have the entire four-year World Treasury Bank MAiN University, top world class course, in Electrical Engineering to be captioned in Bengali. No problem. Maybe he intends to open a 100-student or 1,000-student Electrical Engineering College using the World Treasury Bank MAiN University course. No problem. Proactively, No Copyright by the university.

The DVDs in English cost pennies each, or are free if recorded from the Internet. He can have the captioning done if he wishes by hiring services on the MAiN University site. Or caption it himself, then sell the captioned DVDs, including sell them on the MAiN U site. No problem.

Lectures in English

Noted above is how every course of study under the sun can be captioned in any and all languages, as described.

Yet, it is worth noting that, to most people worldwide, a university education is so difficult or impossible to obtain, that for perhaps a 'billion' people worldwide, to obtain a university degree, by first spending two years or so learning to speak and write English is *not particularly onerous*. Some rich nation citizens may not easily understand this. Moreover, to speak English in today's world, is an intrinsic advantage, including in career. Students can study English for free on the World Treasury Bank MAiN University site. Easy.

It is worth noting that there are 300,000,000 people in China learning to speak English. A Chinese businessman, who made a large fortune with schools that teach English in China, records with pleasure how, when he visited Cuba, everyone with whom he dealt, officials and tourist people, spoke fluent English. Many rural people in China cannot read Mandarin, because they have not learned to remember the tens of thousands of Chinese characters. Some westerners who spend seven long years in China studying Mandarin complain that they still cannot read a newspaper in Beijing.

Second to No University in the World

In every course of study, World Treasury Bank MAiN University policy is to be second-to-no university in the world. That is, World Treasury Bank MAiN University is never interested in being merely 'good enough' or merely 'really excellent'. The Best of the Best is the university's Mission, along with, Always Free.

It may be worth noting that, say for example here, the top computer science professor at Stanford or M.I.T. He may have, say, one-thousand students a year. Yet, at World Treasury Bank MAiN University he can be a world star, and have perhaps *millions of students worldwide*. When he travels in China or Brazil or South Africa, his students may spot him, may be thrilled to see him, and want to get a photo with him.

Also, it can be the policy of World Treasury Bank MAiN Free University to nevertheless pay top dollar. And, although all textbooks *must be free* worldwide online, some students in the rich nations may prefer to purchase the autographed $250 or $500 text book with color pictures and DVDs and all. So the professor at World Treasury Bank MAiN free university may make millions of dollars a year, and drive a Lamborghini and sometimes give lectures to a million students, even millions, worldwide from his glorious beach house in Florida. "Sorry about the sound of those waves crashing in behind me on my beach...." The professor is a bit of a show-off.

Consider the beautiful professor at Harvard who teaches the Core Curriculum essential, The Varieties of Sexual Experience, to 1,000 students. At World Treasury Bank MAiN University, she can be a multi-million dollars a year world star, teaching tens of millions of attentive students, who are seldom late for class. There could be even one-hundred million students, and with physical book and video for sale to the rich kids. Did you see the red short-shorts she wore to lecture yesterday? Hot! The professor may have a twenty million dollar Florida beach pad, where she entertains pretty, pretty boys she calls friends, instead of hanging out in the Professors Lounge at Harvard in January and discussing dreary socialism with depressed professors.

Some may wonder whether World Treasury Bank MAiN Free University might disintermediate other universities and result in their closing.

Our guess is the exact opposite. MAiN University may result in as many as *tens of thousands of new, physical universities*, because the most expensive part of operating a university, the professors, is now free.

We also predict that the world's top universities will advertise that they use the free courses of World Treasury Bank MAiN University as a means of *recruiting students*. Because it can be very inviting to students to participate in classes with millions of online students worldwide, and questions and comments coming in from *every* continent during *every* lecture. A great, compelling experience daily.

A wide variety of new universities can arise. From 100-student, one-course of studies, universities opened by a professor or entrepreneur to 10,000-student universities.

States and towns in poor areas around the world may open their own universities. All of a sudden, rural and poor students from Argentina to Zimbabwe may be studying Stanford-level computer science, M.I.T.-level mathematics, and so on.

Can World Treasury Bank MAiN University have a medical college? Yes, including the cadaver cutting up that is a part of becoming a medical doctor. "Today we will explore this particular lower, bodily orifice...." Each nation, state and province can continue of course to be the sole licensing authority for doctors, as each sees fit. Lectures can be in color, high-definition, and 3D.

Students studying alone can meet up and socialize daily at Starbucks and bars.

World Treasury Bank MAiN University can include esoteric courses of interest to very few. For example, we heard of an online and DVD course on How to be a Sheep Rancher in Utah. There may not be much demand for this particular course of studies, but if World Treasury Bank MAiN University can purchase such courses for a one-time only fee, it can be put on the MAiN University site, under Ranching.

MAiN University will also include vocational courses, such as machinist, carpenter, electrician, nurse, auto mechanic, French cuisine chef, Chinese cuisine chef, and so on. The University can suggest that students take academic courses as well, in mathematics and history and so on.

MAiN University can also offer nation-particularized courses for persons becoming lawyers in India, in Brazil, in Switzerland, in Canada and so on.

World Treasury Bank MAiN University will develop a sea of knowledge on, **How to Build and Operate a Worldwide Free Streaming University**. MAiN University will not regard this knowledge as being proprietary. Most any nation or social group can visit, see the control room with screens of 1,000 simultaneous lectures, sit-in for a year, make notes, meet suppliers, and go ahead with an online, streaming university in their own nation. No problem.

World Treasury Bank MAiN U will also feature twelve years of grade school, at top world level. There may be perhaps ten different K-12 schools in the ten major languages of the world. This can mean that poor people in rural areas worldwide can suddenly enjoy free, grade school education of the quality of top private schools of the rich worldwide.

Some commentators may calculate that World Treasury Bank MAiN University may, by university educating say a billion or even two billion people worldwide, may add trillions of dollars to the Gross World Product.

For World Treasury Bank Founders, thereby being Founders of World Treasury Bank MAiN University, this is to be credited with what is unmistakably, **A historic advance for humanity that will be recognized worldwide, for generations**.
Great, bronze statues of the Founders can be on the campus Great Quadrangle, Forever.

World Treasury Bank MAiN University *carries humanity up from one level to the other*. It ends the class system where only the elite can attend university. It ends the oink-oink Caste System that believes that some normal people are "Not Intelligent Enough" to attend university successfully. This is Pomposity Unchained. Our litmus test is, Any normal person can do the same academic courses as...uh, National Media Television Reporters did in university.
Any normal Black or Brown or Yellow or White kid worldwide can achieve the academic level of, well, admittedly, the Sheer Genius and memorable insights and phraseology, seen in national media television reporters. Brian Williams, Diane Sawyer, clearly Magnificent Intellects for the Ages.

Moreover, as seen in The Real Egalitarianism Section, the classism of only an elite being academically prepared to go to university is ended by humanity's wonderful friend, World Treasury Bank MAiN. The *Real* Egalitarianism is access by 100% of parents to Mandatory School Homework Schools, at top world class level, in which the parent-chosen school takes 100% of the responsibility to supervise that the school homework is done daily. Fun Disruptor Chapters Sixteen through Eighteen.

Any Smartphone Can Be An Entire Streaming University.

There are now smartphones that have in-built projection. This feature is predicted by some to become common. Projection onto any wall, indoors or out, is useful to many occupations, salespersons to foremen and so on.

Projection may prove to be useful here and there to those who wish to use streaming of any course under the sun, sort of like, *Stanford University-in-a-phone.* This might be useful to 'a billion students' worldwide.

World Treasury Bank MAiN University entire four-year courses can be put on tablets. All free. We note the superb Amplify Education, from News Corp, a great corporation.

Any Major Player might see fit to ask himself or herself if there can ever be a greater and more historic benefit to humanity than **World Treasury Bank MAiN's Free Streaming University For All Human Beings Forever**.

Some might reasonably say, 'Curing cancer might be a bigger achievement.' Well, World Treasury Bank MAiN University might cure cancer. MAiN U's to-be huge campus, perhaps the size of Disney World, 25,000 acres, can have any number of research facilities.

Meanwhile, The College of Judaic Studies at MAiN U remains unfunded. Hello! The Yeshiva at MAiN U remains unfunded. Hello!

Sadly, the College of the Study of Chinese Civilization remains unfunded. Alas!

The College of American History....a big hole in the ground. The nation awaits....

World Treasury Bank MAiN University. MAiN U, loved in 200 nations.

Care to be a Founder? It will be an achievement and Legacy for the Ages, for your family and descendants.

A donor, whether World Treasury Bank MAiN Founder or not, can have, "The Your-Name College Of Studies Name" buildings. Your-Name College may have *100,000,000* students daily worldwide.

This could mean that Your-Name College Of **You-Name-It-Studies** could have more influence than most presidents and prime ministers of nations. Forever.

The college can have an eight foot tall, bronze, '2,000 Year' statue of the donor seen at his or her building, architecturally distinguished for the ages. Think, Bronze Statue. You. On the Great Quadrangle of World Treasury Bank MAiN University, viewed by billions.

The above-noted offers a treasure trove of material for You-Tube and Facebook and Twitter entrants in the opportunity to apply for very large awards that might be paid out. Fun Disruptor Awards Chapter Thirty.

Fun Disruptor Chapter Eleven

The Sixth of Twenty-three Currency-Validations by World Treasury Bank that Really Please Humanity.

This is How Billionaires Can Be Acclaimed Worldwide for Decades by Popular, Liberating Actions from World Treasury Bank, the MAiN, and its Founders.

World Treasury Bank will arrange, with Major Media, "10,000" foundations, and 10,000 to 100,000 wealthy families, the Annual-Endowment-Convention in Las Vegas, that we predict will <u>Amaze The World</u> for months and years.

Will the following **Stun the World**? Reader, YOU decide.

THE WORLD PARLIAMENT OF WOMEN

With 3,000,000,000 women worldwide, **voting-by-internet for 500 women Members of Parliament**. And voting for the woman **World Chancellor**. And a woman **Chancellor** elected for each *continent* and for each nation with a billion or more population. World-thrilling. Four-year terms. Elections may be held on the same day or week as U.S. Presidential elections. There can be some Attorneys General in the World Parliament of Women Justice Department. Men, be afraid, be very afraid.

The **Chancellor** can be seen typically surrounded with a guard of 6-foot-6, big-muscled, grim, scowling men guards, scary men with aviator mirrored sunglasses, known as Her-Phalanx. The **Chancellor** should scowl quite a bit herself. Innumerable women worldwide are suffering. She is not called upon to be nice at all. She should not smile as a default expression. When in doubt, be unsmiling. Be a bitch. Seriously. One reference, the ever unsmiling Iron Lady, Margaret Thatcher.

Incredible Buildings

World Parliament of Women is to have Parliament Buildings-for-the-Ages. Capitol Hill-size. London Houses of Parliament-size. With an inspiring, huge clock tower, lit at night.

A huge dome for the Parliament Buildings is a signature necessity. A dome can be very large but architecturally undistinguished. The World Parliament of Women Dome architects will be given as reference points two very beautiful domes, the U.S. Capitol Hill dome with its gorgeous, inspiring triple levels of circles of columns and other uplifting decor, and stunningly beautiful interior natural lighting from windows high in the dome. And, the dome of St. Peter's Basilica in Rome.

Plus, the Basilica *quadruple-deep columns*, the astonishing colonnade around an immense, embracing square. World Parliament of Women must have a quadruple-deep columns colonnade, and the embracing immense square.

Using modern technology and construction, these columns can be brightly lit *from within*, with shifting colors, rather than being mere dumb concrete pillars. Each night there can be truly spectacular light and music shows.

The architects of the World Parliament of Women, Parliament Buildings will be given these parameters: STUN the visitors with the Beauty, and Staggeringly Immense Size, and POWER-POWER-POWER of World Parliament of Women. Bring tears to people's eyes. Especially to women showing World Parliament of Women to their daughters. Kids should be breathless or saying, "Wow" over and over.

Engraved in marble, high-up, BEHOLD THE POWER OF WOMEN.

Around World Parliament of Women Buildings, **acres and acres and acres of outdoor, sylvan garden restaurants, and piazzas like in Rome**. Lunching visitors should say, "This is heavenly. I can't believe how wonderful this is."

A worldwide design competition can begin soon, for world review and critique. One or more Major Players could put up perhaps ten, One Million Dollar Awards to go to the top ten entrants. How about You? Or maybe you *can't afford it*, don't even have the money. This happens. There is no need to be ashamed of your pathetic Poverty. It's okay.

World Parliament of Women's building program will include "1,000,000 BRICKS BUILDING HISTORY", a wall of bricks, each brick with a Brass Plaque bearing the name of the person who has contributed a certain amount to the building of the World Parliament of Women buildings. There can be a searchable database with photos and DVDs of these donors, there for "a Thousand Years". $10,000 per Eternal Brick of History would raise Ten Billion Dollars for the World Parliament of Women Parliamentary Buildings complex. The $10,000 contribution could be paid at $1,000 a year. Middle class women in the rich nations among many others would make the contribution. Men, too. Guys, don't be slugs. Man-up!

World Parliament of Women is to be located on the same '50,000 acre' park as World Treasury Bank MAiN University.

Balmoral Castle in Scotland is on 50,000 acres, about 78 square miles.

The World Parliament of Women can be located in Southern California, or in Florida, to take advantage of a salubrious climate.

The World Parliament of Women Chancellor is to have an official residence, something like a Buckingham Palace, including majestic size, and great public square, like Buckingham Palace Square, called Chancellor's Square, and with beautiful gardens, like Versailles. Buckingham Palace is 108 meters by 120 meters, with 77,000 square feet. (The White House is 55,000 square feet). The idea, upon viewing the Chancellor's Great Residence, people gasp with pleasure at the beauty and size. And, Power.

Chancellor's residence is to have great gardens with dancing fountains lit by colorful LED lights, and also, formal gardens with fountains, with reference to Versailles and Blenheim. Yet, less formal and warmer and more inviting than the great yet coldly geometric gardens of Versailles. And with outdoor restaurants and cafes. Google, Gardens of Versailles. Yet, part of the plan is specifically also to overwhelm touring visitors with magnificent, serene Beauty, and, also with Massively Confident, unapologetic Power, of Women.

Mothers can tell their daughters, "There was The Era Before, for 5,000 Years, when we women were the Second Sex. Then there is this, The Era After, when We As Women wield power Second-to-None. THIS IS WHAT THIS IS." These words will be on a Marble and Bronze Memorial, before which Mothers and Daughters can be photographed.

At the center of Chancellor's Square is to be Chancellor's Column (like Nelson's Column) guarded by a glorious pride of The HUGE BRONZE LIONS, *setting out on the hunt!*

In front of The Great Residence of the Chancellor, the Chancellor's Women's Strict Guard, armed with shiny, silver rifles, marches in strict, stern Parade Ground display, including some marching at double-time, like the Queen's Guard in front of Buckingham Palace.

Perhaps a shiny gold armored personnel carrier hourly rushes onto Chancellor's Square. Armed women Guards jump out, ready for action.

On the grounds, a Statue of Liberty-inspired **Statue of Woman Holding Up The Globe**. Liberty is 151-feet tall, about 15 stories, and twice that height counting the base. So, too, Woman Holding Up The Planet. Even 500 feet? Cologne Cathedral is 516 feet. Washington Monument, 555 feet.

For both solemnity and fun, inside the stunning Parliament Buildings, there can be a raised, marble-floor circle, 50-to100-meters in diameter, where ONLY WOMEN AND GIRLS MAY BE HERE, with The Women-Only Gates onto The Great Gold Circle. The floor may be shiny, looking like 'solid gold'. Dad can take pictures of mother and daughters.

There can be the feature around **The Great Gold Circle: The Eternal Hand-held Candle Flame**. There is *always* a woman holding a lighted candle. Sometimes hundreds of women holding lighted candles. Any woman inside The Great Gold Circle lights the candle of a woman who is stepping inside the Circle and of her daughter. The Eternal Hand-held Candle Flame. A perpetual, emotionally moving ceremony. Young daughters, entranced, and never-forgetting.

A replica of the huge Office of the World Chancellor, a World Power Office, will be there for mothers and daughters to sit behind the Huge Power Desk and have a photo taken. The daughters won't forget that.

Like World Treasury Bank's MAiN University, free university for all human beings forever, World Treasury Bank MAiN's World Parliament of Women *raises up all human beings forever. This is a major advance in civilization. It carries humanity up from one level of development to another.*

It is a historic advance for humanity. **It is for the ages.**

Will you be involved? Men, ask your wives. Follow orders.

World Parliament Of Women will stream interactive Internet TV channels in many languages.

All of this stands to give women worldwide some 'Male Swagger' in their personas.

World Parliament of Women Will Exercise Very Serious, Major World Power

Most boycotts are ill-conceived, strategically inept, and are merely the public affairs of resentment or pouting. However, it is worth noting that a popular, economic boycott can be *a power second only to mounting a major military invasion*. The creation of the United States itself was trip-wired by a major boycott against the superpower of the time. The Mahatma Gandhi-led boycott forced the great Empire to do what it could not even conceive of doing, leave India. The Montgomery Bus Boycott compelled the then power structure to do what it dearly did not want to do and said that it would "Never" do.

World Parliament of Women can arrange a boycott of all of a nation's products by the world's women, and thereby a boycott by the women's families. That is, a boycott by billions of people. This is an actual, facts-on-the-ground, *exercise of very serious world power*. It is an immense threat.

This is, **Women breaking through to the Other Side in wielding World Power**. Women autonomously, without help from men, without consulting with men. Some observers may suggest that this is the first time ever.

Examples of Liberation and Power for Women

Consider that The World Parliament of Women decides to boycott a nation due to its systematic oppression of women, and rape being not investigated, and gang rape unpunished. A worldwide economic boycott of the nation is threatened beginning on a date not far off. This may well cause the nation's economic elite to go to the federal legislature, and insist that laws and practices be changed. "We have to prosecute these crimes against women now. That's the new thing."

The threat can be buttressed by seven-figure, eight-figure, nine-figure and ten-figure-a-*day* fines until: crushing-economic-boycott-if-necessary.

A key requirement by World Parliament of Women will be that every police station in a nation that oppresses women must have a women police officer on duty as desk officer, 24/7, to receive criminal complaints from women. She must be armed with sidearms that she is *required* to use to protect women, including protect women from male police officers, a common crime in some nations. A woman seeks to lodge a complaint about having been gang raped. The police detain her to gang rape her themselves, sometimes for days. There is no prosecution.

The woman desk sergeant must be visible though the front door window. A large neon sign must read, Women Lodge Criminal Complaints Here to Women Police Officers.

All such changes must be audited by women of the nation reporting daily to the World Parliament of Women, reporting about any police station that does not have such an armed women desk sergeant. And reporting in turn to major media worldwide. And featured on World Parliament Of Women's streaming Internet TV channels, worldwide in many languages.

Not less than fifty percent of the presiding, and sentencing, judges in crimes against women must be women.

World Parliament of Women will pass 'legislation' and insist on increased and severe criminal penalties for trafficking girls and women, and for rape. Rapists are being coddled.

World Parliament of Women candidates for a Parliamentary Seat must pledge to all other women in the world that they are willing to prosecute crimes against women. World Parliament of Women Attorneys General and Justice Department will be major powers.

A Key World Parliament of Women Requirement Can Be

That prison sentences for crimes against women be audited by women armed with sidearms. Because otherwise even the minimal, insulting-to-women prison sentences are not served. The criminal deserves 30 years. He gets a year. He is out in a few months. "It's only women."

Sexism pervades the legal system in India. – Wall Street Journal, May 17, 2013. For unbelievable example, women are still being pushed into marrying their rapists, by caveman, knuckle-dragging judges. Criminal judges, in our view.

These matters can be reported on a World Parliament of Women web site. National legislators will be talking about this.

The World Parliament Of Women is to be an app from World Treasury Bank MAiN in the World Treasury Bank smartphone download. The app can be in *the major one-hundred languages of the world*. What does this mean? What this means is that **a truly major, world-stunning, historic advance in human civilization and real power for women occurs overnight**.

The Whole World Changed, in One Day.

The World Treasury Bank MAiN app will include the Smart-phone, Internet Voting Software. This is the Internet voting set-up for 2,000,000,000 growing to 3,000,000,000 women worldwide. This means that the World Parliament of Women could be up and at them with stunning speed, in great buildings in Florida, pending the building of the above-noted Parliament Buildings for the Ages.

The World Parliament of Women's **Department of Justice** will give full jurisdictional respect to each nation that does not have women in it.

Women need to be empowered to unapologetically "break through to the other side" in wielding real power. This happens in the World Parliament of Women.

Will the World Parliament of Women **Stun the World**?

The above-noted World Parliament of Women is another very substantial reason for 1. The major Internet corporations, and 2. One or more or all five major U.S. media corporations, to be involved in World Treasury Bank MAiN <u>with your click-through logo</u> on the World Treasury Bank site home-page.

The above-noted offers a treasure trove of material for You-Tube and Facebook and Twitter entrants in the opportunity to apply for very large awards that might be paid out. Fun Disruptor Awards Chapter Thirty.

Fun Disruptor Chapter Twelve

The Seventh of Twenty-three Currency-Validations by World Treasury Bank MAiN that Really Please Humanity.

This is How Billionaires Can Be Acclaimed Worldwide for Decades by Popular, Liberating Actions from World Treasury Bank, the MAiN, and its Founders.

THE EMANCIPATION PROCLAMATION FOR ALL WOMEN WORLDWIDE

The Emancipation Proclamation for All Women Worldwide is to be an app from World Treasury Bank in the World Treasury Bank MAiN smartphone download, in *the major languages of the world*. The app includes the Internet voting set-up for 2,000,000,000 growing to 3,000,000,000 women worldwide.

What this means is that another, truly major, world-stunning, historic advance in human civilization occurs *Overnight*.

The Emancipation Proclamation for All Women Worldwide can be partly written online. The clauses can be general, yet with specific supporting clauses.

For example, a key clause must be Freedom of Movement. Yet, this freedom must be supported with various, specific, autonomy clauses for adult women.

A key clause must be The Right to Lethal Self-defense. A few years ago there was a sensation in an African nation of women killing their brutal husbands in self-defense. Woman bites dog. You go girl.

Though women being armed with pistols may not appeal to all, the recent developments in '3D printing' of pistols (that is, laying down layer after thin layer of carbon composites and other materials, to make desktop pistols) might be embraced by some women around the world, who need lethal self-defense against pitiless brutes. What will the World Parliament of Women have to say about this? Maybe they will set up 3D printing in some nations where women are brutally treated. Men, be afraid, be very afraid. Ref., Ready, Aim, Print, Economist, February 14, 2013.

A clause will be Freedom of Sexual Expression by adult women.

The Emancipation Proclamation for Women Worldwide app can be, in every smartphone, in one-hundred languages. The major languages are, 1. Mandarin Chinese (1.1 billion), 2. English (330 million; 1 billion+ including English as a Second Language), 3. Spanish (300 million), 4. Hindi/Urdu (250 million), 5. Arabic (200 million), 6. Bengali (185 million), 7. Portuguese (160 million), 8. Russian (160 million), 9. Punjabi (130 million), 10. Japanese (125 million), 11. German (100 million), 12. Javanese (80 million), 13. French (75 million), German, Korean, Hebrew, Turkish, Italian, Ukrainian, Vietnamese.

The above may mean: **Billions of Women in 200 nations and states in strong support of World Treasury Bank MAiN**. Happy women. This is another very substantial reason for the major Internet corporations, and the noted major U.S. media corporations, to be involved in World

Treasury Bank MAiN with your click-through logo on the World Treasury Bank site home-page. And perhaps on every one of 2-to-3,000,000,000 pages of the Bank's account holders.

The actions herein that help billions of people may thereby outflank, disarm, and neutralize critics of World Treasury Bank *private-sector* issuance of the MAiN.

These actions can perhaps be part of some Major Player individuals and firms achieving triple-digit billions in wealth. Fun Disruptor Chapter Eight. It may also be worth considering the effect of the above-noted major, historic advances, for one's reputation, and legacy for one's family.

Women major players should step up. Make yourself known. Don't smile.

The above offers a treasure trove of material for YouTube and Facebook and Twitter entrants in the opportunity to apply for very large awards that might be paid out. Fun Disruptor Awards Chapter Thirty.

Fun Disruptor Chapter Thirteen

The Eighth of Twenty-three Currency-Validations by World Treasury Bank MAiN that Really Please Humanity.

This is How Billionaires Can Be Acclaimed Worldwide for Decades by Popular, Liberating Actions from World Treasury Bank, the MAiN, and its Founders.

That predictably there will be queries from the U.S. Treasury and the Federal Reserve

The new currency, the MAiN, is not to be a replacement currency for any other currency. Yet, out of an abundance of caution, the Plan seeks to respond to perhaps overreaching by federal regulators.

CONGRESS TV CHANNEL

World Treasury Bank will convene Major Media friends and others, and *overnight* create **Congress TV Channel**.
Congress TV Channel is not a channel about Congress.

RATHER: Congress TV Channel gives to each member of Congress, in unchanging, untradeable, alphabetical order, a 15-minute, 'Say and Show Anything from Anywhere in the World' TV newsmagazine. Seen on worldwide television.

This is 96, 15-minute segments per day, (24 hours times 4 segments per hour).

For <u>each</u> Congressman and Congresswoman, A - Z, this is his or her, **Say and Show Anything to the Nation and to the World from Anywhere on Earth** newsmagazine during the 8 hours between 4 PM and midnight, 32 segments.

This is a 15-minute Evening Segment <u>every 16 days</u> – for <u>each</u> member of Congress. (535 members divided by 32, 15-minute segments during eight hours every evening).

The plan is that there be, even if unnecessary, two minutes per TV newsmagazine for sponsors. Sold in advance, to finance the channel.

Also, Congress can easily appropriate funds for Congress TV Channel. This would be popular. Alas, the habits of modesty and humility and frugality make this appropriation unlikely.

In total, there is a 15-minute segment <u>every 6 days</u> for *each member* of Congress, A – Z. That is, 535 members of Congress divided by 96, 15-minute segments in each 24 hours.

Congress members like this. Really REALLY want this. But they will stop short of publicly running over cute kittens to get it. There is a limit. Maybe.

Congress TV Channel can be emulated around the world. There can be Parliament TV Channel, U.K. Parliament TV Channel, France. Parliament TV Channel, European Union. Parliament TV Channel, India. Parliament TV Channel, Brazil. Parliament TV Channel, Canada. And so on.

A member of Congress or a lobbying firm could purchase this book for distribution to every member of Congress. Similarly, for every member of Parliament in the U.K., European Union, India, Brazil, and in every other nation.

WHILE AT IT, the Plan is that two other channels be created overnight: **Democratic Party TV Channel** and **Republican Party TV Channel**. We just want to be loved. It is good to be loved. Because love is power.

The idea is that these two channels are of, by and for each political party. Democratic Party TV Channel and Republican Party TV Channel are best in identical studios, side-by-side, in D.C. For love. Love is a many splendored thing.

Side-by-side also helps greatly in getting good 'gets', major interviews. For examples, the visiting Prime Minister of Britain may be more likely to visit Democratic Party TV Channel if, after giving an incredibly brilliant interview, he can walk through a covered walkway to the Republican Party TV Channel, and give an equally incredibly brilliant interview. Brad and Angelina, Jay Z and Beyoncé may more likely visit Republican Party TV Channel if they can pass by the Prime Minister under the Walkway-of-Fame to Democratic Party TV Channel. We love Beyoncé. She can lip sync all she wants.

The plan is that these three channels be side-by-side on the cable channel listing, and at the lower end in channel numbers. That is, say for examples, Channels 33, 34, 35. No, not 147, 173, and 249. The three channels are a necessary Public Service. We suppose that the Majority Leader might "just happen to mention", to any slow-witted media executives, a genial plan to re-assign the owned-and-operated Station Licenses that are on The Public's Airwaves. Suddenly, quick-witted. Brilliant!

Ordinary Fortune 500 lobbying and AFL-CIO lobbying is to creating **Congress TV Channel** and **Democratic Party TV Channel** and **Republican Party TV Channel** as ping pong is to NFL football. Members of Congress could and should move mountains overnight to get these three channels *overnight*.

SUGGESTION: Call the chief executives of the major media corporations. Invite them all to a meeting, or "invite" them all to **Weekly Progress Meetings**. Offer your patriotic reflections on the owned-and-operated Station Licenses that the Public owns on Their Airwaves. Secure a **Date-Certain**. To avoid "accidental foot-dragging".

Major Players and Fortune 500 corporations and major unions should get behind World Treasury Bank MAiN's overnight creation of Congress TV Channel and Democratic Party TV Channel and Republican Party TV Channel. For love. Love is important. Because love is power.

Back to considering Congress TV Channel

Members of Congress can fly to anywhere on earth to make their 13-15 minute video for their next A to Z time slot. It can be worth noting that the three-day workweek is common on Capitol Hill. Indeed, some rude people, people without manners, even say that it is more like a 2.5 day workweek.

Congress Member: "Here I am in northern Canada, where we see these magnificent polar bears...."

Congress Member: "I am here in Sudan, at a factory where weapons are being manufactured to be transshipped for the sole purpose of killing Israelis. Therefore, I will introduce a Bill in the House to....."

Congresswoman: "I am here in Dhaka in Bangladesh at the school for these girls...."

Black Congressional Caucus Members: "We are here outside this high school in South Side Chicago. We are here talking to boys who are just leaving at the end of the school day, which we note with great, great dissatisfaction is only 2:00 PM. We are also very, very unhappy with what these fine boys are telling and showing us about their *No-School-Homework* situation. There is no success in grade school education without Mandatory School Homework. *This No School Homework regime is the destruction of a prosperous future for millions of Black families.* The graduation rate for Black males in Chicago is 39 percent. Camera, stay with us as we go into the school and confront the principal about this horrible, national scandal....."
Hispanic Congressional Caucus Members, same thing.

Congress Member: "I am here at this school in Singapore and finding out why it is a lot more successful than far too many of our schools back in America....."

Congresswoman: "I am here in Los Angeles with Janet, who is 15, and who has been streetwalking this block for a year. We are going to rescue her. Here comes her very angry-looking pimp who, to his surprise, is going to be arrested as he gets here....."

Congress Member: "Here we are with beleaguered Christians in Iraq....."

Congress Member: "I am here in a U.S. Navy nuclear submarine that I cannot name, under an ocean that I cannot name..."
Congress Member: "We see here these glorious wild horses here in Oklahoma...."

Congress Members: "We are here on the campus of the University of _____ to confront university administrators about the clearly anti-Semitic three-day event held here last week...."

Congress Members: "Today let's look again at how much a $20 Trillion National Debt is. We have as a guest here a one-year-old baby."

Congress Member: "Meet the family that won my Weekly Puppy Dog Giveaway. Is this a cute puppy or what?"

Lobbying firms can create 15-minute scripts for review by members of Congress. These need not be and often should not be limited to the lobbyist's immediate concerns. The Congress TV Channel video newsmagazine might be credited, 'Created by Name-of-Lobbying Client'. Just a thought.

These three side-by-side channels, Congress TV Channel, Democratic Party TV Channel, and Republican Party TV Channel, mean <u>535 Friends in Congress</u>. Friendship is good. Friendship is power. Power is friendship.

The creation of these channels is Historic, Big Time Lobbying.

A PROBLEM: World Treasury Bank Founders may be being called by 535 Members of Congress to offer praise to the Founders. Consider the critical danger of being admired too much by members of Congress. "Call me anytime if I can be of help. Here's my smartphone number..."

One must bear the burden of power, somehow.

Our prediction is that the ratings of Congress TV Channel, and DNC TV and RNC TV may.... surprise network TV news.

The above-noted offers a treasure trove of material for You-Tube and Facebook and Twitter entrants in the opportunity to apply for very large awards that might be paid out. Fun Disruptor Awards Chapter Thirty.

Fun Disruptor Chapter Fourteen

The Ninth of Twenty-three Currency-Validations by World Treasury Bank MAiN that Really Please Humanity.

This is How Billionaires Can Be Acclaimed Worldwide for Decades by Popular, Liberating Actions from World Treasury Bank, the MAiN, and its Founders.

AN ADVANTAGE FOR ALL HUMANITY, ESPECIALLY WOMEN: WALKING-TALKING ROBOTS

Walking-Talking Robots, with"human appearing" faces and hands, stand to change the world beneficially for all human beings more than the automobile and electricity. Walking-Talking Robots may become as large as the automobile business worldwide. Each family member may have his or her own Walking-Talking Robot.

For example, parents may want each child to have his or her own Walking-Talking Robot as babysitter-protector to walk their young children to school, and to keep an eye on the child at the playground.

The Walking-Talking Robot can stream video back to the parent's smartphone or Google Glass in real time. The Walking-Talking Robot (WTR) can wait outside in the sun or rain or snow for the end of the school day. No problem. Robots have infinite patience. Robots work for free. Robots never get tired.

The number of automobiles in the world has surpassed one billion. There may be more than a billion Walking-Talking Robots in time.

More reasons why Walking-Talking Robots may become as big a business worldwide as the automobile business:

Walking-Talking Robots (WTRs) give every human being the great luxury that previously only kings, queens, dukes, princes, princesses and the Super Rich have enjoyed: PERSONAL SER-VANTS. That is, Personal Butler Robots.

For examples to your Walking-Talking Robots, with human-appearing skin and eyes and hands (these already exist). You have named your two robots, **Rock** and **Susan**.

Rock is... handsome, sort of. Susan is... not bad looking:

"Susan, go upstairs, bring down my red, my green, my yellow, and my blue sweater. I'll choose one."

"Rock, I'll sit in the Starbucks patio. Go get my coffee and croissant at the counter. Ask them if they have that new coffee from Borneo. Pay with my World Treasury Bank card."

The Starbucks baristas *greet your robot*, "Hi, Rock! How's it going?" They like Rock. Rock is never rude.

Rock returns and sits down. "Rock, what is the square root of 23,030,401?" Rock gives the answer in *one second*.

"Susan: Wash the car. Do the laundry. Mow the lawn. Walk the dog. Clean the house. Wash all the windows in the house.

"This evening: Take the bus with little-Johnny to his soccer game, beam your Internet telecast going-and-coming and of the game to me. Broadcast my cheers for Johnny."

"Rock, walk to the mall. Buy me a new beach towel and tele-cast the selections to me. Then go the supermarket and pick-up 20 pounds of potatoes, then walk to the dry cleaners and pick up all of our dry cleaning. Walk home. If a fire starts, call 911 as you grab the children, clear the house, phone me, and video stream to 911 and to me."

It is two AM. "Rock, thanks for waking me about the ominous sounds downstairs. Burglars or rapists are in the house. Go check it out with your array of weapons, as you silently call 911 and Internet-stream everything to the police."

Rock is way, way beyond fearless. Rock is bulletproof. 'His' artificial hands can squeeze 500-1,000 pounds pressure on the rapists' arms, until the cops come. OUCH! Rock can turn on two big red lasers pouring out of his 'eyes'. Scary.

The two robber-rapists downstairs shoot Rock three times. The bullets bounce off Rock. Worse for the home-invaders, Rock bursts into loud, room-filling laughter. Rock can shoot rubber bullets that can knock over and hurt a large man.

Rock holds the two home-invaders until the police come. While holding the criminals, Rock makes sarcastic remarks about their lack of manliness. The 6-foot-2 criminals whimper and plead with Rock not to hurt them. When the police arrive, Rock hands over the criminals with the remark, "Take these puppies." Puppies! Your personal World Treasury Bank MAiN Walking-Talking Robot refers to brute criminals as 'puppies'.

People will love their robots like friends.

Response to YOU once-a-day by your Walking-Talking Robot to this catalogue of endless, tedious labor: "A pleasure to be of service to you. I hope that you have other tasks for me." Robots do not need to be paid.

Robots in Japan and South Korea now have "skin" that, at first glance, looks like human skin, "eyes" that look like human eyes, human-looking "hands" with fingers with joints, and articulated thumb. They 'shake hands' with visitors and talk and listen to people.

Robots can now squeeze a peach with tactile-sensing. Homes, washing devices, kitchens, and so on, can be made robot-friendly, including with radio-frequency chips everywhere. There is video of a robot folding towels, a difficult dexterous task. Many a wife can't get her husband to fold towels. No problem. Susan loves to fold laundry.

Finally: "Would you like to dance?" A Honda robot can dance to music now. Geek dance. Bust a move is coming.

People will pay a monthly license fee to have their Walking-Talking Robot look <u>exactly like Denzel or Halle Berry</u>. Denzel sends his Daily Voice: "Advancing your life today? Tell me how." You sit at Starbucks chatting with Halle who says, "You better see my new movie and rate it great or we won't be having our daily chat." Uh oh. Better do what Halle says.

Declining neighborhoods may be reborn, empowered, and prosperous due to Home-Protector and Person-Protector robots. Thugs...give up the thug's life and....go get jobs. Walking-Talking Robots may make the thug's life most unpleasant. Every woman and mother and home made safe. Every child safe to-and-from school with his <u>Watch Over Me</u> Walking-Talking Robot servant. Like having as many cops as people.

Go camping in the wilderness. Totally safe with Rock standing grimly outside your tent all night. There can even be robots with the strength to shatter the legs of an attacking bear. Three young women find themselves in a campground with some unsavory looking men. No problem. Rock the Robot, your personal armed policeman on duty 24/7, your personal King Kong guard. *No one* would dare bother the girls.

Opportunity to Be Involved

Major Players who may become involved in World Treasury Bank MAiN can be involved in what may become an immense worldwide business that humanity greatly enjoys. A theme of this book is that Major Players can be in a business that benefits billions of people worldwide.

The Plan herein is that the first or second year of the annual Money Summit, in Beijng or Singapore or Wellington or Dublin or wherever, will include, **The Annual World Walking-Talking-Robot Makers Convention, from World Treasury Bank MAiN**. The convention can include all robot makers for all purposes, industrial robots and so on, yet with the Mission of Walking-Talking, Personal-Servant Robots for all.

Moreover, the Convention will invite the development of hundreds of items to be specially-compliant for Walking-Talking Robots. The idea is to encourage the development of WTR-compliant smartphones, refrigerators, door locks, microwaves, point-of-sale terminals, homes for the handicapped, lawnmowers, washing machines-and-dryers, frozen dinners, police partners, and etcetera and etcetera unending.

Including homework helpers. "Now let's do quadratic equations. It's easy."

The World Walking-Talking-Robot Makers Convention might be held twice a year, say in Las Vegas and Beijing.

Perhaps worth noting in passing, major annual conventions may be sold unto themselves for a billion dollars. Comdex sold for $800,000,000 in 1995. The World Walking-Talking-Robot

Makers Convention might have its own Initial Public Offering for ten figures.

A Major Player could purchase a copy of this book for each Major Player in his or her Rolodex, and send it with a cover note, perhaps along the lines of, 'Please get back to me if you are interested in this....'

In our biased view, being "not interested" in The World Walking-Talking-Robot Makers Convention is like Henry Ford asking his neighbor in 1908 if he wants to buy into the Ford Motor Company. The guy says, "No, Henry, I'll stick with Dobbin. Horseless buggies are a fad." Poor fellow.

Walking-Talking Robots stand to change the world beneficially for all human beings more than the automobile and electricity have done

Women Liberated from Fear

The particular beneficiaries of Walking-Talking Robots may be women in regards to security against male violence and fear of that 5,000-year scourge against women. All of a sudden, every woman has the equivalent of a 6-foot-4, 250-pound policeman strapped-to-the-max as her personal protector, in the form of a cute Walking-Talking Robot companion, yet who can fearlessly, casually take care of a bunch of criminals.

The Turn-On-Turn-Off glaring, red lasers from his eyes, the ominous, grim, 'Don't mess with *Me*, chump' demeanor cause strong men to look away.

The above-noted offers a treasure trove of material for YouTube and Facebook and Twitter entrants in the opportunity to apply for very large awards that might be paid out. Fun Disruptor Awards Chapter Thirty.

Fun Disruptor Chapter Fifteen

The Tenth of Twenty-three Currency-Validations by World Treasury Bank that Really Please Humanity.

This is How Billionaires Can Be Acclaimed Worldwide for Decades by Popular, Liberating Actions from World Treasury Bank, the MAiN, and its Founders.

A MAJOR ADVANCE FOR WOMEN IN SPORTS

World Treasury Bank MAiN can convene the **MAiNGlobal Football League from World Treasury Bank MAiN**, as a means of obtaining incalculably large free advertising as Name-Founder and Sponsor. Football here refers to what is known as Soccer in America. With success, the 'free advertising' can continue for years and even decades.

Also, a theme of this book is that Major Players in finance can make yet more money while pleasing literally billions of people worldwide. Happy people, a good thing.

The suggestion here is merely about a world sport, yet *a team sport in which women athletes can play on the field with men*, and which may be watched by huge numbers of families worldwide.

The MAiNGlobal Football League is a Historic Breakthrough in Sports

The sprint speeds of women in such as the 100-meter and 200-meter races and so on have become very close to men's speeds. Football requires endurance, sprinting for 90 minutes. In these regards, a woman from Belarus won the Los Angeles Marathon overall in 2013.

She even beat the Kenyan guys. Then the sky fell in.

Herewith the proposal: that <u>The MAiNGlobal Football League from World Treasury Bank MAiN</u> be formed by a group of Major Players, for example, those among the Founders of World Treasury Bank MAiN.

There may be, say, 40 teams, from *The Largest Cities On Earth*. Each major nation may get perhaps five or more teams. Each team must own, not lease, its own trans-ocean jet, say the Gulfstream 650. Scheduling may as a matter of course allow two teams to share a jet.

Herewith the breakthrough for women on the team sports field: **Each team must have not fewer than two women players on the field at all times**, as running position players, as differentiated from the goalkeeper. This means *every mother and daughter on earth can watch with fascination and pleasure and pride.*

Showbiz is part of this League

Games might be played at night, for maximum special effects with lighting.

The ball is to be fired onto the field by a loud 'cannon' that is *atop the stadium*, instead of being placed on the grass by that skinny guy in short pants.

Each woman player on the Home Team is to wear a shimmering, actually glittering, brightly reflecting Gold Uniform. Each woman player on the Visiting Team is to wear a shimmering, actually glittering, very bright, reflecting Silver Uniform.

The jerseys on all the players are to be, believe it or not, lit from within, including with blinking lights. Each jersey can feature advertisers. When a player scores a goal, stick out your chest with your blinking-ads jersey.

It gets worse from the standpoint of football purists. The League will have an average of three goals per game, averaging one every 30 minutes during 90 minutes. If there are fewer goals in a year, the size of the goal will be expanded for next year, say, made wider by two meters, and higher. If more than three goals per game are being scored in season, the size of the goal will be reduced for next season.

Each goal scored will cause the whole goal area, and *the entire stadium*, to be lit up and blinking to huge musical accompaniment. The fans sing at top lung, "We are the champions......"

If it turns out that headers cause brain damage, the closed-fist hitting of the ball will be allowed. Maradona of 'Hand of God' fame, told us that the fist works great for scoring, when the referees aren't looking. A header or 'fist' may count for two goals. Fist-goals may be better theatrically than headers in any case.

The ball itself must be colorfully lit from within. This feature alone may bring English Premier League executives to tears.

Our friend Nick jokingly suggested the following outrage to propriety, indeed an Assault Against All Civilization itself: that there be *Two* balls on the field at all times. This would be chaotic excitement. The Plan here is to give this crazy idea a Top Secret tryout, with big armed guards keeping out all sports reporters. History will absolve us!

If this unbelievably bad idea unexpectedly works, the Goal-keeper will have a six-foot-long/two meter, lit-from-the-inside, flat bat to aid him when facing Strikers that are moving the two balls into his territory, like a Panzer invasion.

As a final assault on good sense and propriety, and even against basic brains, during the last 15 minutes of each game, a sideline row of orange stage flames may erupt from containers along the length of both sidelines, say three feet high, behind a protective fence. When the game clock hits 90:00 minutes, the flames will go out, except if there is overtime.

Each team may become worth a billion dollars, or more. Real Madrid is worth $5.3 billion and takes in $650 million in annual revenues, and has 50,000,000 Facebook and Twitter followers.

The League may give the winning team players money awards after each game. The award cheques can be given to each player immediately after the game, on the field.

Wagering will be encouraged as allowed by law. Wagering is to include the popular-with-legislatures, Beneficial Automatic Individual Retirement Account. Bet $10.00, put down $11.00. This 10 percent goes into his or her Beneficial Automatic Individual Retirement Account. And betting is by Debit Card only. No credit cards.

IN SUMMATION, The best thing of all: the historic break-through, up from 5,000 years of single-sex only team sports, of <u>men and women athletes on the field together</u>. Mothers worldwide... watching their young daughters react as *a woman player leaps up high amidst twenty leaping-up men*, and scores a 'Hand of God' fist goal in chaotic action. Wow!

Some of these women players may not be exactly delicate damsels. Look for young women from the slums of Sao Paulo, Jo'burg, Shanghai, Chicago, Cairo maybe, with muscular legs, and who have three brothers with whom they have engaged in the occasional fist fight.

Five Major Benefits for Women Worldwide

World Treasury Bank MAiN offers five major benefits to every woman worldwide:

The World Parliament of Women. An immense, historic breakthrough.

The Emancipation Proclamation for All Women Worldwide.

World Treasury Bank MAiN Free University for All Human Beings, Forever.

Walking-Talking Robots, which among innumerable benefits for all, can end 5,000 years of women being victims of, and intimidated by, the male capacity for violence against women.

Of lesser order, the MAiNGlobal Football League breaks 5,000 years of women being seen as not able to play any athletic team sport with men. Great for growing daughters to see.

The above-noted offers a treasure trove of material for YouTube and Facebook and Twitter entrants in the opportunity to apply for very large awards that might be paid out. Fun Disruptor Awards Chapter Thirty.

Fun Disruptor Chapter Sixteen

The Eleventh of Twenty-three Currency-Validations by World Treasury Bank MAiN that Really Please Humanity.

This is How Billionaires Can Be Acclaimed Worldwide for Decades by Popular, Liberating Actions from World Treasury Bank, the MAiN, and its Founders.

FOR PREPONDERANT, UNPARALLELED INFLUENCE ON CAPITOL HILL

AN OPTION: World Treasury Bank can make known that it can, at will, offer a download app to 100,000,000 American voters to download 10,000 to 20,000 MAiN each, perhaps worth $10,000 each, or perhaps not, to thereby, overnight, sign-up 100 million voters, loaded for bear.

All this striking, nation-amazing action would cost "only" one to two Trillion MAiN, amidst perhaps 100 Trillion to be issued over some years.

An additional option would be to found, Suuuper!Party! in the U.S. via the same app downloaded from the World Treasury Bank site. Suuuper!Party! could have, perhaps, 50,000,000 to 100,000,000 voters.

Suuuper!Party! could be the, um, well, The Largest Political Party <u>literally overnight</u>. Is this a... Big Deal?

What do You think?

Suuuper!Party! will not be a third party. Third is the way of all folly in America. RATHER: The Party would *nominate solely the Presidential candidate of either the Reps or the Dems*, the day after the second of the two conventions. Thereby, Suuuper!Party! could enjoy an unmatched, daily, major influence in *any* U.S. administration regarding regulators. This is much more influence than any third party could obtain by fielding its own, outlier candidates.

1,000,000 Block President Couples

The noted Suuuper!Party! app can also sign-up 1,000,000 or more Block President couples. *This is one couple for each and every block in America in all 50 states.* Each couple can have their website overnight, for their block or apartment house.

"We can bring over vote-by-mail forms, if you like."

"Do you need a ride to the polls? What time?"

"Thanks for the coffee and cookies the other day."

This would make Suuuper!Party! more organized than the other two political parties combined.

Is this significant in politics and power? Whatever.

What are your views?

Suuuper!Party! would thus accrue very large weight in both parties and presidential candidates, and in *any* U.S. administration, and <u>neutralize and outflank overreaching regulators</u>. Suuuper!Party! respects the important, proper duties that regulators are given to do. But overreaching, not so much.

Each candidate would simply *require* the Suuuper!Party! nomination to win the election, and say so publicly, including in every election campaign debate. Both candidates say, "I definitely want the Suuuper!Party! nomination, and I intend to get it."

Suuuper!Party! will be able to work closely with the President regarding all nominations to the Cabinet, Bureaucracy, Judiciary and Diplomatic Service. Also, chairman of the Federal Reserve, and U.S. Treasury Secretary.

World Treasury Bank may insist that treasury bank/central bank disbursements are properly tax-free. Earnings by MAiN would of course not be tax-free.

The Purpose served by the above-noted: *to neutralize any opposition better than any amount of lobbying that can be obtained.*

The Arrival of The Black Swan

Suuuper!Party! is a modern, friendly name, like Yahoo! and Google and Apple. Adults and kids can have fun drawing out the 'uuu' as oo-oo-oo. Suuuper!Party! may become **suddenly the most powerful private institution in the nation**, a Black Swan event, predicted by no one.

What do You think? Is this huge?

Yet, <u>all the above is a seemingly-bad idea because</u>: People disagree about politics. Therefore, any dubiousness that the reader feels is well-grounded.

HOWEVER, 80% of the Suuuper!Party! platform by weight would be the 1. *Politically neutral*, 2. Ingenious, 3. Attractive, and 4. Compelling, Real Egalitarianism.

Suuuper!Party! alone has the Real Egalitarianism.
See if you like it:

Real Egalitarianism is: access by 100% of parents to Mandatory School Homework Schools, beginning at grade one, at *top world class level*, in which the parent-chosen school takes 100% of the responsibility to supervise that the school homework is done. For this reason, Suuuper!Party! takes a special interest in the appointment of the Secretary of Education.

Suuuper!Party! means to end the hapless, feckless, Never-Going-To-Happen idea that success in grade school education is about "inspiring the children to learn". One problem with this unreal, candy floss notion is that it excludes ninety-nine percent of boys. The reason for this is the following: They are Boys!

IQ Does Not Measure Intelligence

The IQ test merely measures what generation you are in the Mandatory School Homework Culture. There is: The Not Yet Generation. There is the First Generation: he stumbles through college. There is the Second Generation: did well at university. There is the Third Generation: Advanced academic degrees in difficult disciplines.

There is the Fourth Generation: I have decided that I am, basically, a Genius. So far, his wife has not noticed. He makes so many simple mistakes. To her, he often seems none-too-bright.

IQ measure intelligence? This is a ridiculously pompous notion. Intelligence in any normal human being is deep, broad, with daily lightning flashes. Every Nobel Prize winner thinks of three...really dumb ideas every day. Every university professor has had high school dropouts explain some things to him on occasion. "Oh, I get it now, at last, now I see," says the professor to the auto mechanic dropout.

Ref., The Genius in All of Us: New Insights into Genetics, Talent, and IQ. – David Shenk.

Great Teachers Are Not a Solution to Improving Education

A majority of teachers are, by definition, going to be *average*. The system must de facto compel average teachers to end up with strong results. Like, um, nursing. Like, uh, accounting.

Moreover, in America today, the term great teachers usually means super-caffeinated, devoted, haplessly deluded young women, racing around the classroom like nutty masters of ceremonies, and blind to boys. Their futile endeavor: the current sad, depressing, quicksand, silliness about "inspiring the children to learn". These teachers usually burnout after a year or two. Whereas, with The Historic Civil Rights Act for Real Egalitarianism, and The Sixteen Basic Guarantees to Parents, they could have extraordinarily rewarding careers. Fun Disruptor Chapters Seventeen, Eighteen.

When the boys leave the school room, they are not talking about Plato's Philosophy. They talk about such as teacher's big bum. Inspired? Boys?? Fuggedaboutit.

Suuuper!Party! articulates, and fills, a huge and heartfelt desire for egalitarianism, that *no other political party* does. For preponderant, unparalleled influence in the nation:

The REAL EGALITARIANISM, REAL EQUALITY is –

That 100% of all parents must have access, beginning at Grade One, to an actually-mandatory Mandatory School Homework School, at Top World Class Level, that <u>takes 100% of the responsibility for supervising that the school homework is done, five times a week, 200 times a year, for 12 years</u>.

Just like the rich man's private boarding school for his son.

Relentlessly, every school day for twelve years, the boy who 'forgot' to do his homework last night, is held in detention after school, to do school homework under stern, suspicious, super-vision, from the first days of Grade One to the last week of Grade Twelve.

The RESULT: He 'hates' school homework, but *he grinds it out for 12 years*, as he is compelled to do. 2,400 assignments.

He <u>goes to university</u>. Girls, too, of course, but if school is set up to work for girls, many boys fly under the radar screen, or worse. Whereas, if the ordinary orderliness and discipline of the school keeps boys in line, this usually works for girls.

That is, they study every night. They go to university.

On top of the attractive distribution of 10,000 MAiN to each of 100,000,000 voters that may be worth $10,000 each, Suuuper!Party! would <u>stun and paralyze the old politics</u> with the compelling, electrifying, nation-arousing assertions, seen here that,

"No parents in America, in all 50 states, in all 3,100 U.S. counties, can find a Mandatory School Homework Public-School for their children. Yet, there is no success in Grade School Education, and many fewer chances in life, and uni-versity often denied, without Mandatory School Homework Schools. This is the biggest domestic crisis and scandal in our nation since 1860."

The above-noted offers a treasure trove of material for You-Tube and Facebook and Twitter entrants in the opportunity to apply for very large awards that might be paid out. Fun Disrup-tor Awards Chapter Thirty.

Fun Disruptor
Chapter Seventeen

The Twelfth of Twenty-three Currency-Validations by World Treasury Bank MAiN that Really Please Humanity.

This is How Billionaires Can Be Acclaimed Worldwide for Decades by Popular, Liberating Actions from World Treasury Bank, the MAiN, and its Founders.

THE PUBLIC SCHOOLS EMPEROR HAS NO CLOTHES

No American parent in all 50 states can find a high school in which there is *not* Mandatory Practice on the Sports Teams.

School homework is equivalent to practice. Mandatory practice in sports is like wearing clothes. It is universal. Parents educated and not educated, assume it.

A son who comes home and complains to his parents that the coach read him out and made him run around the field or court backwards, while his teammates smirked and laughed, is *universally* told, "Of course, practice is mandatory. Your team would lose every game big time if there was no mandatory practice. Show up on time in future. Practice hard. Make us proud. Do what the coach says." This is called, NORMAL.

Yet, some readers with cardio problems might see fit to be seated before reading the following sentence, the most stunning sentence in this book or perhaps any book this year:

No parents in all 50 states can find a Mandatory School Homework School among the 100,000 public schools in America. This is such a startling assertion, that some people may need a few moments to mull it over. It is as startling as asserting, "No parents in all 50 states can find a school at which the students wear clothes." America does not have the latter problem. It has the immense crisis and scandal of the former problem. There are different types of nudity.

Consider that parents in South Korea, Taiwan, Hong Kong, and Singapore cannot find a public school where school homework is *not* mandatory. This is called, NORMAL.

Most any public school principal in America will claim to an inquiring reporter, "Of course, school homework is mandatory at this school. It is an outrage to claim otherwise." Let us now translate this claim into English.

Here is the translation: "We assign school homework. We tell the students that it must be done. *Therefore, they must have done it.*" History is super-abundant with really dumb remarks. But the latter is one of the dumbest remarks ever.

Further delving into the depths of The Public Schools Emperor Has No Clothes epic, nation-stunning scandal, the claim that there is mandatory school homework means, "Of course we do not check whether the school homework is done. Parents who are professionals and successful, relentlessly force their sons and daughters to do oodles of school homework every night. All others are left to sink, because, in all honesty, *they are not bright enough.*"

So, after 5,000 years of every civilization and culture that has ever existed, including some immensely incompetent cultures and worse-than-incompetent cultures, the teachers unions and educrats and their allies have revealed to the world the Utterly Unique Unbelievable Theory (UUUT) that, Children Do Not Require Supervision (CDNRS).

This is Supra-Incompetence. This is addle-brained ignorance. This is denial of human nature. It is part of the War Against Boys that is seen throughout America's public grade school system. One result is that annoying, disruptive boys become annoying, disruptive men. And worse. The War Against Boys is the title of a book by Christina Hoff Sommers. Charlotte Allen notes of the book, in the Wall Street Journal, June 26, 2013, "...the K-12 education system that feeds into college favors docile, conformist girls over aggressive, competitive boys."

As many a commentator has noted, if the U.S. had been militarily occupied, we would call what has been done to the U.S. school system an 'Act of War' against the U.S.

Welcome to the biggest domestic scandal and crisis in American history since 1860.

This is the wrecking of a prosperous future for Black America every school night.

This is the wrecking of a prosperous future for Hispanic America every school night.

This is the wrecking of a prosperous future for Blue collar and Pink collar America every school night.

This is the wrecking of a prosperous future for much of White suburban America every school night.

Depending on a legislator's or commentator's persona and preferences, alternate words than the above 'wrecking' that one might use are: Disempowering. Cheating. Grievously harming. Limiting. Hurting. Destruction. Assassination.

Many people, actually many, many people think the following: that *Parents* should supervise that their children, ages 5 to 18, do their school homework, five times a week, 200 times a year, for twelve years, totaling 2,400 Parental Supervisory Assignments of a difficult, slippery, high-stress, mutual misery-causing task that confuses both parents and children.

There is a problem with this formula. The problem with this formula is that it has never remotely worked, in any field of human endeavor, for the past 5,000 years. The idea that the government, in this instance the school system and the Department of Education, is to advise parents who were not mandatory school homeworked themselves when they were in school, that they should somehow do, five-nights-a-week, complex, frustrating, stress-filled supervision that often results in raised voices, and family unhappiness, 200 times a year, for 12 years, 2,400 difficult assignments, is unreal. It is totally unreal. It is unconnected to the reality of how real-flesh-and-blood humans live their daily lives.

It has never happened in history.

It is like saying that new cars should come in 2,400 parts, to be assembled by the buyer.

Whereas, the efficient, intelligent way to do car sales is to give to the automobile buyers, a fully assembled car, with all 2,400 parts already put together. Brilliant!

Equally brilliant: Offer to parents, beginning at grade one, Real Egalitarianism, the Real Equality, access by 100% of parents to Mandatory School Homework Schools at top world class level, in which *the parent-chosen school takes 100% of the responsibility to supervise that the school homework is done.*

The method of course, simple and easy for school principals and teachers who have Probity and Gravitas, is to check school homework individually each morning, and relentlessly hold students in detention after school if they did not do necessary school homework last night.

The Growing Inequality in America

The growing inequality in America is not due to Wall Street.

The growing inequality in America is not due to the one percent most prosperous.

The growing inequality in America is not due to the big banks. Nor is it due to corporations.

The growing inequality in America is not due to "millionaires and billionaires."

All of the above build prosperity in America. They are all great.

The growing inequality in America is not because we do not spend enough money on grade school education. America's schools are Fat, Fat, Fat with money, including Inner City schools. Newark spends up to $24,500 per pupil each year. At twenty students per class, that is rounded $500,000 per class room. Huge. Yet, even if it was $5,000,000 per classroom, or *even $1,000,000-per-pupil,* it still would not be enough.

There can *never* be enough money because of the hapless, tragic, self-hobbling of the Cartoon-Land Despotism of **No Mandatory School Homework**, a despotism imposed especially over Black and Hispanic families, and Boys.

When the teachers unions assert to legislators that more money is needed to improve the schools, Congressional and Statehouse legislators should bluntly insist on cuts. Parents will understand.

If Newark cut its budget per pupil from $24,500 to $10,000 or less, fired all the teachers, and brought in Korean Women school teachers from Seoul, and instituted daily-audited, Mandatory School Homework, **Newark schools would be the best in the nation**. Come on, Cory Booker. Man up! Your problem is that you went to Yale Pantywaist U. You need a graduate course in De-Yaleification. Perhaps Bruce Springsteen would do an 'intervention'. The Boss is a skilled De-Yaleifier. The Boss will have you singing De-Yaleification songs with him, possibly on stage. Brilliant!

The growing inequality in America is due to the collapse of the grade school system, to the, here is our nation-shaping refrain, *the wrecking of a prosperous future for Black America every school night, the wrecking of a prosperous future for Hispanic America every school night, the wrecking of a prosperous future for Blue collar and Pink collar America every school night, and the wrecking of a prosperous future for much of White suburban America every school night.*

As noted, Commentators and Legislators who might prefer less dramatic terminology than wrecking can replace the word wrecking with such as, Disempowering. Cheating. Grievously harming. Limiting. Hurting. Disemboweling.

In any case, the solution is the Real Egalitarianism: access by 100% of parents to Mandatory School Homework Schools, at top world class level, in which the parent-chosen school takes 100% of the responsibility to supervise that the school homework is done.

This solution has the attractive feature of being free. It is cheaper to run a Mandatory School Homework School than one with the disciplinary problems and chaos of a No Actually-Mandatory Homework school.

If America fired 100% of school teachers, and replaced them with women school teachers from South Korea, Taiwan, Hong Kong, and Singapore, parents would be delighted at the results. The only unhappy social group would be the prison guards. The prison guards would be asking, "Where is our weekly and monthly and annual influx of young Black males and Hispanic males and lower-middle class and poor white males? Our tears are flowing. What is this crap about mandatory school home-work? Hello! We need our pensions."

The Compassionaters

It is good to be compassionate. Unfortunately for some foolish 'compassionaters', they decline to recognize for other people's children the fact that, **There is no such thing as helping Lower Middle Class and Poor families rise up without Mandatory School Homework Schools**. This does not exist. It never has. Everything else is true Classist Oink-oinkism. It is White Southern Paternalism writ large to Black, Hispanic, and lower middle class whites.

"I am intelligent. The people that I am helping are not." This is what the compassionater thinks. He glows with his compassion. He puffs up proudly, so proudly with his Brutal Compassion, with his Pathological, Airhead Altruism. Meanwhile, he thinks this Classist, Caste System, Porker idea, "My children are intelligent, university material. Your children are not intelligent enough to do the university work that, for example, national media television reporters did."

We have a question: how come his wife never talks about how intelligent he is? He often seems kind of slow on the uptake.

They are compassionaters.

The Real Egalitarianism, guaranteed to parents, needs to be legislated.

Parent-Chosen

The Sixteen Basic Guarantees to Parents

Parent-chosen, Mandatory School Homework Schools appeal to both university educated parents, and, to parents who are self-admittedly clueless, and *scared*, and thoroughly intimidated, about supposedly supervising 2,400 mandatory school homework assignments. Mandatory each night. For 12 years. Intrinsically a fantasy idea.

These parents, the huge majority of parents, can barely imagine doing such supervision. These parents are thrilled and delighted to have such school choice, beginning at grade one. They know. They *know*. Better, their Mandatory School Home-worked sons and daughters behave better at home.

Real Equality in a parent-chosen, Mandatory School Home-work School, means the Real Egalitarianism Program seen below, The Sixteen Basic Guarantees to Parents.

Black and Hispanic leaders among others should grimly, unsmilingly, avoiding chuckling, about *a subject that is as serious as Stage-Four Cancer* in your communities, and **insist on The Historic Civil Rights Act for Real Egalitarianism**.

Here are the Act's **Sixteen Basic Guarantees to Parents:**

1. One hundred percent of parents must be offered access, beginning at grade one, to an actually-mandatory, Mandatory School Homework School, at top world-class level, in which the school takes 100% of the responsibility for assuring that homework is done 200 times a year.

2. In every Mandatory School Homework School, from the early days of Grade One to the end of Grade Twelve, mandatory school homework is assigned Five Times a Week.

3. The next morning in class, each student's homework from the night before, is checked *individually*. Not always by the home room teacher. No showing of hands. One after another, the students have the presiding teacher examine their work from the night before. This takes less than a minute per pupil.

All reading assignments include one or more pages of composition. The homework must be presented in tabbed order of subject. It can be flipped through. Or tablet-summary examined.

4. If proper homework has not been done, or not done acceptably, ("No, this is messy. Completely unacceptable. You will have to do it over in detention after school"), the invariable result is detention after school, an hour for little kids, two hours for big kids. No excuses about school bus schedules. Sorry!

One result: even kids criticize the friend who gets held after school in detention. They say to him, "Just do the homework the night before. Just get in the habit. Then we can hang out after school." The detention room must be teacher-supervised from the first minute to the last. The reason is well known to those teachers who have become adults.

5. **The Parental right to Benchmarking Comparisons**: The daily school homework assignments in Singaporean schools, or equal to these schools, will be posted online, five times a week, 200 times a year, for 12 years, 2,400 times for every parent and teacher and reporter to compare. Moreover, the 2,400 *video lessons* as taught by Singaporean teachers must be available to every student and parent online. English is the language of instruction in Singapore.

This benchmarking, these comparisons with world leaders in grade school education, cause great fear and trembling in the U.S. teachers unions, and in the U.S. Department of Education. They are the stark naked, bare bum, Emperor who wants to be told, "Your robes are beautiful, Your Majesty."

6. Parents must have the right to class action sue the school board *overnight*, from parent-chosen law firms listed on the school board web site, sue for modest amounts, say $10,000

per household for failure to abide by The Sixteen Basic Guarantees to Parents. The law firm is paid by the school system to: immediately deliver to the school a blunt, Cease-and-Desist Letter with Demands-for-Proof Within 72 Hours.

For example, Keyshawn and Jose and Bubba were not required to do mandatory school homework last week. The school would be given 72 hours to prove this horrific, Class System, Caste System accusation to be wrong. Otherwise, the school board has to pay up within 30 days. That the parents can effortlessly sue *overnight* and at no cost is major empowerment against Classism, against the oink-oink, often racist Caste System of education. Conscientious teachers can be glad that the system outflanks their colleagues who are feckless or Caste System Pompous.

7. Each student has the right to smartphone video the teacher daily checking his or her school homework. To show to parents, and law firms.

8. The right to be taught each subject solely by teachers who have a Masters Degree in that discipline.

9. The parental right in coed schools for not less than 50% of the teachers, in each grade, specifically including each of grades one through six, be 'manly men'. Manly means only that grade school teaching by men not become the preserve of 5'5" men with receding chins who talk about their Scrabble scores. Boys need some stern, imposing, frowning, manly men teachers.

10. Parents must be offered the choice of coed schools, and all girls schools, and all boys schools. Some boys, some girls, thrive best in a single-sex school. Parents decide.

Vouchers to 100% of parents. Each summer, each school can invite parents in to convince them to use their vouchers at 'our' school for the next school year. All the schools compete each year to get the voucher money that is attached to each student. As in Singapore. 'Here is what we can do for your child.'

Charter schools welcome to any degree.

Some boys thrive only in an atmosphere of tall, broad-shouldered men who may carry bullhorns and who never need to speak a certain sentence during twelve years of school, because the boys understand the unspoken sentence, "You want to go fist-city, tough guy, let's go fist city."

The boys *love* this, including little boys. They thrive *academically* in this atmosphere. "Did you see his hands?? They are the size of pie plates!" The boys ages 5-18, enjoy this. They are smiling, and, are forced to hit the books. Thereby they go to university. Possibly they attend the free, top world class, World Treasury Bank MAiN University.

11. All teachers at a Mandatory School Homework Schools must sign a pledge agreement that the formula, "inspiring the children to learn", fails to get most children to do school homework, especially boys.

12. There is no tenure. Tenure institutes incompetent and burned-out teachers. It sacrifices children.

13. All pensions are to be solely by teacher contributions. No surprise bills to the taxpayers twenty years later for hundreds of billions of dollars. People are no longer willing or able to be presented with enormous tax bills from Top Secret Contracts made a generation ago. Contracts without the to-be Payer's knowledge are not valid.

14. Overall positive view of American history.

15. The U.S. Constitution taught. It is the Constitution of our nation. Who knew?

16. Shakespeare taught in high school. The Bard is a Universal Common Denominator.

Teachers unions and educrats are facing the Quad Co-ordinated Lawsuits. The Quads are joint lawsuits by the U.S., by all 50 states, by every U.S. school district, and by 100,000,000+ American victims of the teachers unions' incompetent, oink-oink, Classist, Caste System, culture. Fun Disruptor Chapter Eighteen herein. Let us discuss. Let us reason together. We just believe in courtesy and respect, to us from others.

The above means that hybrid, **Suuuper!Party!-Democratic candidates and Suuuper!Party!-Republican Candidates Shatter the Caste System in Grade School Education.**

They shatter the caste system, after 5,000 years of, 'We are intelligent. They are not'. Pompous! Boring!

The above-noted offers a treasure trove of material for YouTube and Facebook and Twitter entrants in the opportunity to apply for very large awards that might be paid out. Fun Disruptor Awards Chapter Thirty.

Fun Disruptor Chapter Eighteen

The Thirteenth of Twenty-three Currency-Validations by World Treasury Bank MAiN that Really Please Humanity.

This is How Billionaires Can Be Acclaimed Worldwide for Decades by Popular, Liberating Actions from World Treasury Bank, the MAiN, and its Founders.

THE HISTORIC CIVIL RIGHTS ACT FOR REAL EGALITARIANISM

Suuuper!Party! insists that any White House candidates who want the Suuuper!Party! nomination, or Congressional Democratic or Republican Party hybrid candidates with Suuuper!Party!, fully support, and will sign on television, **The Historic Civil Rights Act for Real Egalitarianism, Year 20__**. This means: access by 100% of parents, beginning at Grade One, to Mandatory School Homework Schools, at top world class level, in which the parent-chosen school takes 100% of the responsibility to supervise that the school homework is done, five times a week, 200 times a year, for twelve years, 2,400 Mandatory School Homework assignments.

INATTENTIVE PARENTS, NO PROBLEM. Their kids are going to go to university anyway. The parents become delighted parents.

The Historic Civil Rights for Real Egalitarianism includes each and all of The Sixteen Basic Guarantees to Parents. Fun Disruptor Chapter Seventeen.

The Real Egalitarianism law requires that, in parent-chosen Mandatory School Homework Schools, beginning at grade one, there be *daily auditing individually,* not weekly, not monthly, not twice a year, that the school homework is actually done, and that, *thereby, lower middle class and poor families are not cheated out of Actual Egalitarianism.*

Their children go to university.

The Real Egalitarianism equally requires daily, online benchmarking, 200 times a year for 12 years, comparisons with Mandatory School Homework assignments with top world class school systems, such as Singapore. This is the shattering of The Caste System in the U.S. that is composed of: Real education for the Upper Middle-Class, and the sacrifice of all others to the hapless, despotic, ruthless, pitiless, ignorant, Lords-Lording-it-over-the-Dumb-Peasant-Children despotism of No-Mandatory-School-Homework-Schools.

Free at last! Free at last!

So they are all off to university, perhaps World Treasury Bank MAiN University, free university for all human beings forever. Thanks to World Treasury Bank MAiN Founders. This is also, oh, say 50,000,000 to 100,000,000 **voters who will not vote any other way**. Lower-middle class and poor parents *know*. They *know*. Classist condescension is over. Pompous asses helpless.

Some school teachers will like the above and perceive it as what it is: Liberation, and Elevation, and Empowerment for the teaching profession. Others, not so much.

The Historic Civil Rights Act for Real Egalitarianism, Year 20___ is a supra-gigantic winner for the Democratic National Committee, 202-863-8000, and for the Republican National Committee, 202-863-8500. The case can be made that such liberating legislation *remakes American politics* and liberates many tens of millions of families.

Hey, here's a great idea Mr. Major Player: Send a copy of this book to every member of Congress, with a note suggesting that he or she look at Fun Disruptor Chapters Seventeen and Eighteen. Costs not much. May make history. Note that **all 535 Members of Congress will *totally love* Congress TV Channel and Democratic Party TV Channel, and, Republican Party TV Channel**. Suggest Fun Disruptor Chapter Thirteen.

The American people want the teachers unions and educrats to be confronted due to their omissions that cause so much harm to American families. So much disaster for American families. So much catastrophe for American families.

And the gutting of Black America.

Those teachers who see the liberation and elevation for *teachers* in the Real Egalitarianism, should step up. "Every middle-class and poor family can double its income in this generation." RNC, DNC, go for it.

Innumerable organizations should embrace **The Historic Civil Rights Act for Real Egalitarianism, Year 20___**. Organizations such as the NAACP, Rainbow/ PUSH, Hispanic organizations, and so on.

The Historic Civil Rights Act for Real Egalitarianism, Year 20___ is clearly **the most important civil rights legislation in decades**.

The smartest man in America, Thomas Sowell, tsowell.com, points out, "Recent statistics on the students who passed the

examination to get into [the elite] Stuyvesant High School ....
included 9 black students, 24 Latino students, 177 white students, and 620 Asian Americans."

The Solution to this grotesquely unnecessary inegalitarian-
ism, *the solution to this assassination of Black America every
school night* and this keeping-down of Latino and Blue Collar
America is: the Real Egalitarianism of access by 100% of parents to Mandatory School Homework Schools at top world
class level, in which the parent-chosen school takes 100% of the
responsibility to supervise that the school homework is done,
five times a week.

Many major business leaders speak on venues such as
CNBC about the need to "fix" America's failing schools. When
these powerful chief executives speak on this problem, they
look *helpless*, and *pleading*. They are helpless. They are helpless before the U.S. and 50 statehouse departments of education, and the teachers unions' ghastly, incompetent, goofy-land,
No-Mandatory-School-Homework-Schools.

No-Mandatory-School-Homework Grade Schools are like
birthday cakes without flour, without yeast, without icing, and
without candles.
No-Mandatory-School-Homework Grade Schools are like a
huge Mercedes-Benz, with no engine.

Business organizations such as the Chamber of Commerce
and the Business Roundtable should adopt and lobby for the
inherently, *hugely popular*, **The Historic Civil Rights Act
for Real Egalitarianism, Year 20___.**
When it is a *Universally Known Fact* that There is No Success in Grade School Education Without Actually-mandatory,
Mandatory School Homework Schools, The Historic Civil

Rights Act for Real Egalitarianism, Year 20___ makes singularly attractive public affairs that benefits all Americans, and stands to lead the world. Other nations may emulate.

Delight America

Potential candidates for the White House should formally adopt in their platforms **The Historic Civil Rights Act for Real Egalitarianism, Year 20___** and the awe-inspiring, vote-cascading language of the Real Egalitarianism.

Include the hugely enjoyable, **The Sixteen Basic Guarantees to Parents**. Fun Disruptor Chapter Seventeen. You will get landslide votes.

Consider these words in every presidential campaign speech and television debate, as said by this or that Presidential candidate that *You,* the reader, like:

"America needs the **Real Egalitarianism**, the Real Equality. Because right now, there is, the *wrecking* of a prosperous future for Black America every school night.

"There is the *wrecking* of a prosperous future for Hispanic America every school night.

"There is the *wrecking* of a prosperous future for Blue collar and Pink collar America every school night.

"There is the *wrecking* of a prosperous future for much of White suburban America every school night. That is, there is no success in grade school education without Mandatory School Homework, audited every day.

"There is not to be found in these United States even one public school that offers, to parental-choice, a Mandatory School Homework School. Yet, 99% of parents would choose Mandatory School Homework Schools, given the choice at grade one.

"THIS SCANDAL IS ONE MILLION TIMES WORSE THAN THE WATERGATE SCANDAL. Really. America is being horribly injured (alternatively: Disempowered. Cheated. Grievously harmed. Limited. Hurt. Assassinated) by a failed school system."

Your Presidential candidate saying the above. Work well?

1,250,000 People Gather On the Washington Mall

Speech remarks, as above-noted, by Democratic and Republican party candidates for the White House and Congress, can *move the nation.* Crowds expected to be 5,000 turnout to be 25,000, then 50,000 and, soon enough, fill the Washington Mall. Historic.

Mr. Politician, Mr. Legislator, Ms. Legislator, will you be on the dais when the Washington Mall is filled with 1,250,000 people, on a nationwide, historic telecast, seen worldwide?

But are they intelligent enough?

Some people may ask, or rather, many, many people ask, Are the sons and daughters of lower middle class and poor Black Americans, Hispanic Americans and Blue collar and Pink collar Americans "interested in" university education.

This question is almost always a polite way of asking a rude question. Here is the Classist, Caste System, Oink-Oink, rude, crude, actual question: Are the sons and daughters of lower middle class and poor Black Americans, Hispanic Americans and Blue collar and Pink collar Americans *Intelligent Enough* to do academic school homework and, later, university studies?

The good news is that in the past 5,000 years, of the innumerable social groups that have been judged to be "not intelligent enough" or the rude "stupid", not one has proven out.

NOT ONE. The Victorians in China discovered that the Chinese simply could not be taught mathematics. That judgment has proven to be....incorrect.

Most of today's American brilliant scientists, engineers, professors, tycoons, surgeons and so on are the descendants of European peasants who literally did not know their left foot from their right foot. (Army drill instructors would put a straw in the boot of the left foot. Farm boys at least knew what a straw was. The drill instructor would bellow out marching orders for hours, "Straw foot, right foot, straw foot, right foot...."). Brilliant!

That farm boy's great grandchild is an electrical engineer at Oracle.

Some farm girls, from a certain Emerald Isle that shall be nameless here, upon becoming household maids, when first confronting a staircase, tried to ascend it on all fours. Their employers taught the girls how to go upstairs using only their legs. Brilliant!

That girl's great granddaughter is a computer scientist professor at Stanford. And she ascends stairs using only her legs. Brilliant!

How, then, did the descendants of these Hapless Boob Men and Don't-know-anything-about-anything Women miraculously become the brilliant scientists and mathematicians and self-made billionaires and presidents of the United States? The Sole and Universal answer: at some point their parents, or luck, led to *The Great Secret of Moving Upwards*, Mandatory School Homework Schooling.

President Obama recalls that when he was a schoolboy in Hawaii, his economist father, visiting at Christmastime, instructed his son to go into his room and do school homework. Young Barack responded that as this was Christmas vacation, there was no school homework. His father insisted that Barack do as directed. This Mandatory School Homework regimen seems to have worked out okay for Barry.

Sean Hannity of Fox News recalls that when he would come home from school and claim to his mother that he had no school homework, his stern Irish mother would have none of that. She required the young Sean, future $100 million dollar man, to sit at the kitchen table and do work from each and every textbook.

Hannity has a sign in his office from the bad old days, Now Hiring, No Irish Need Apply. It seems that certain hod carriers from the Old Sod habitually spilled cement. They have since learned to keep the hod level, thus not spilling the cement. Brilliant!

Bill O'Reilly, another $100 million dollar man, recalls that he was given three solid hours of Must-Be-Done-or-Be-Doomed school homework every night at Chaminade High.

The late U.S. Senator Patrick Moynihan co-wrote an entire book about how the Irish at long last discovered that "you really have to push your kids in school."

Translation: Mandatory School Homework five times a week for twelve years.

Mandatory school homework, five times a week, two-hundred times a year, for twelve years, also helps families to be intact. The male from the single-mom home, stabilized by the Mandatory School Homework-Going-to-University regime, resolves to marry his girlfriend (after both get their Masters Degrees) and be a father to their children, born after graduation.

The Quad Co-ordinated Lawsuits Will Delight America

Legislators who confront, or who are confronted by, the teachers unions and school boards can just so happen cheerfully to mention the Quad Co-ordinated Lawsuits.

Quad Co-ordinated Lawsuits are joint lawsuits by the U.S., every U.S. state, every U.S. school district, and '100,000,000' American victims against the incompetent, Classist Despotism, Lords-Lording-Over-the-Dull-Witted-Serfs, Caste System culture of the educrats and the teachers unions.

The nation will love these class action lawsuits with passion. With glee. And high-fiving. And by voting for the Quad Co-ordinated Lawsuit candidates against the teachers unions candidates for Congress and statehouses.

Quad Co-ordinated Lawsuits can be for Fraud and Misrepresentation. And, Malfeasance with hundreds of billions of dollars of public money, due to the wrecking of a prosperous future for Black America every school night, the wrecking of a prosperous future for Hispanic America every school night, the wrecking of a prosperous future for Blue collar and Pink collar America every school night, and the wrecking of a prosperous future for much of White suburban America every school night. That is, 'There is no success in grade school education without Actually-Mandatory School Homework'.

Just as there is no success on high school sports teams without actually-mandatory practice, before a stern and unyielding coach. Coach is famously not a jokey-pie guy. He frowns. He shouts. He intimidates and he means to intimidate. He is dealing with boys. There's a big problem right there.

Members of Congress and state legislators who seize this nation-stunning issue will be hugely *empowered*, and *loved*, and *voted* for, by the American people. The huge majority of parents were not mandatory school homeworked themselves when they were in school. These parents are *inwardly heartsick and helpless* as they see their own children limited, and even going wrong, and their family being grievously limited.

They *know* that Mandatory School Homework Schools are a *necessity* and are a healthy normality.

Trayvon Martin would be alive today, deciding what university to attend, exchanging daily pleasantries about the Miami Heat with George Zimmerman, if his parents had had access to Mandatory School Homework Schools.

Thanks, teachers unions.

To end the public's heartsickness about *NOT-BEING-ABLE-TO-GO-UP* is to gain huge vote totals.

Votes for progressives. Votes for conservatives.

As it is known worldwide that, <u>There is no success in grade school education without actually-mandatory Mandatory School Homework Schools</u>, we suggest that, among others, Black leaders and Hispanic leaders, hold fun discussions at which the word 'education' is banned. The reason is that the world education has become increasingly vaporous in America and often in Britain. The idea here: the word education has four syllables. If you can say four syllables, you can say four words. Instead of the word education, say Mandatory School Homework Schools. We suggest, put a jar in the center of the conference table. A person who uses the word 'education' instead of saying Mandatory School Homework Schools, puts in $100 for the Party Fund. Just for fun.

Major Players, major law firms, the NAACP, Rainbow/ PUSH, Urban League, Latino organizations, the Congressional Black Caucus, the Congressional Hispanic Caucus, Protestant, Catholic and Jewish groups should gather together and launch the world-stunning, world-admired Revolution Against Caste, also known as, the Real Egalitarianism, the Real Equality: the Real Egalitarianism of access by 100% of parents to Mandatory School Homework Schools, at top world class level, in which the parent-chosen school takes 100% of the responsibility to supervise that the school homework is done. Launch the world-stunning Quad Co-ordinated Lawsuits.

One idea: take out full-page announcement ads, 'let us gather together', in the Wall Street Journal. For Class Action Lawsuits. And, to advocate passage of the actually supra-historic, **The Historic Civil Rights Act for Real Egalitarianism, Year 20___**. It will be worldwide news, celebrated.

Get Paid Big Time

Black and Hispanic organizations should and must receive double-digit millions and triple-digit millions in Apology-Remorse Payments in the Quad Co-ordinated Lawsuits settlements. These groups can be civil rights organizations, NAACP, Rainbow/PUSH, and also the National Black Chamber of Commerce, Latino organizations, 100 Black Men of America, Center for Neighborhood Enterprise, Black fraternities, women's groups, and so on.

It is absolute Suuuper!Party! policy that these Apology-Remorse Payments be paid. Suuuper!Party! alone created **The Historic Civil Rights Act for Real Egalitarianism, Year 20___**. And, **The Sixteen Basic Guarantees to Parents**. And the **Quad Co-ordinated Lawsuits**. Suuuper!Party! stands by and insists on major Apology-Remorse Payments.

BP has had to pay out high double-digit billions of dollars for the, comparatively, minor damage of the oil spill. Very minor damage in comparison.

Members of Congress, including say the Congressional Black Caucus, who find that they are not being shown proper respect by the teachers unions, can, oh, just cheerfully mention the idea of a federal government custodial arrangement of the teachers unions, due to Fraud and Misrepresentation. And due to Malfeasance with hundreds of billions of dollars of public funds. Malfeasance with public funds is a federal, state and local crime. This is willful, caste system, malfeasance that is *the destruction of a prosperous future for Black America every school night, the destruction of a prosperous future for Hispanic America every school night, the destruction of a prosperous future for Blue collar and Pink collar America every school night, and the destruction of a prosperous future for much of White suburban America every school night.*

The Excitement of Contract Law

In Contract Law are the reasons for the coming, inevitable, U.S. and 50 statehouse and 3,100 county school boards and 10,000 other school boards, and 100,000,000 parents and Voters in Class Action Lawsuits for fraud, misrepresentation, and malfeasance by the educrats and the teachers union recipients of immense federal and state education funds.

Contract law requires Full Disclosure of all material facts in *any* contract. And, good faith and fair dealing. *The teachers unions have never, ever disclosed to their employers that they have not the remotest clue of how to set up even one Mandatory School Homework School anywhere in these United States.* Not one among 100,000 schools. Nor have they any intention whatsoever of setting up even one Mandatory School Homework School anywhere in these United States. Innumerable books will be written of the ghastly damage caused. The savaging of Black America.

The teachers unions were required, and are required today, absolutely obligated, in Contract Law, to say to the U.S. Department of Education, to each U.S. state and to each school board in America, just before signing their contracts, "Oh, incidentally, we have no idea whatsoever of how to set up even one Mandatory School Homework School anywhere in these United States. We also have no intention whatsoever of setting up even one Mandatory School Homework School anywhere in these United States, as this might injure the self-esteem of brat boys."

The U.S. and the 50 state legislatures, and the 10,000 U.S. school districts would have responded, "Thank you for your Full disclosure, as required by Contract Law. We will not sign the contract under any circumstances. Good-bye. Please leave, you must. Don't contact us. Go ahead and strike if you like. No problem. We will hire teachers from the millions of retired professionals, few of whom suffer from your self-enfeebled, seriously creepazoid inability to set up Mandatory School Homework Schools in the United States of America, which is this nation. Consider getting psychiatric help to try to solve your deep, deep and bizarre problems."

Congress Members and Statehouse Legislators Empowered

Trillions of dollars in Would-Have-Been Wealth has been destroyed in the Black and Hispanic and Blue collar and Pink collar population by the current teachers unions complete, historically amazing inability to set-up even one, actually-mandatory, Mandatory School Homework Schools anywhere in these United States.

From Maine to Hawaii, from Alaska to Key West: NOT ONE. A vast, tragic desert. The Sahara Desert is like the Great Lakes compared to the teachers unions' Caste System Desert.

Home Ownership for All

The best way by far of getting people into home ownership is by empowering them with Mandatory School Homework Schools. The case can be made that much of the financial crisis of 2008 arose from paternalistically putting No School

Homeworked people, that is, Low Income people, into homes that they could not afford, with resultant trauma to millions of families when they lost their house. The pain of such trauma lasts for decades, especially in children. The topic is worth a major book unto itself.

The fraud, misrepresentation, and malfeasance, the malfeasance with hundreds of billions of dollars of public money by the teachers unions and educrats, might well result in indictments, by the U.S. Department of Justice and U.S. states Attorneys-General.

It is a simple, blunt fact that malfeasance with public funds is a consequential crime. The nation awaits developments.

This horrific betrayal of America is actually much *worse* than the above-noted haplessness. For the unstated Classism, the Caste System awfulness is that the teachers unions believe, in documents, that, prepare yourself, perhaps sit down before reading the following nightmare horror sentence:

"The sons and daughters of lower-middle class and poor Black American parents, Hispanic American parents and Blue Collar parents are **Not Intelligent Enough** to do the same academic work in high school and university as was done by a pointed litmus test: national media television reporters."

Thus it is that the teachers unions have brought this disaster upon themselves. This is a self-wrought catastrophe from the mistakes that human beings in power always make. Pride. Arrogance. Classist and Caste System assumptions of superiority. Racial assumptions of superiority.

They also drown cute little puppy dogs each weekend while laughing fiendishly, as they in actual fact drown tens of millions of the sons and daughters of lower-middle class and poor Black

American parents, Hispanic American parents and Blue Collar parents, and solidly middle-class, white suburban families, each school year under **the social waterboarding of No-Mandatory-School-Homework schools**. Millions of Black American families have been shattered, destroyed by this lordly, Dukes surveying their serfs, Caste System arrogance and incompetence.

The "at risk" young Black man standing on the street corner is much brighter and sharper than the European peasant of old, whose great grandchildren are engineering professors at M.I.T. Exactly how intelligent is that "at risk" young Black man? He is as intelligent as national media television reporters see themselves as being. And he could have done the *exact same* studies that they did in school and at university. No problem.

But he is tragically doomed by the teachers unions' Caste System. The prison guards await his arrival.

Thanks, teachers unions.

The above-noted three, suicidal words, *NOT INTELLIGENT ENOUGH* is the epitaph on the career gravestones of those who live such low-rent, cornball, pridefulness. Some people are indeed *Not Intelligent Enough*. But it is not the sons and daughters of the American people.

This situation empowers America. We can now obtain **The Historic Civil Rights Act for Real Egalitarianism, Year 20___** of access by 100% of parents to Mandatory School Homework Schools, at Top World Class Level, in which the parent-chosen school takes 100% of the daily responsibility to see that the school homework is done. By holding "I forgot" boys after school in stern, supervised detention. This method is known worldwide. It is considered to be NORMAL. The American people say, "Give us The Historic Civil Rights Act for Real Egalitarianism, This Year."

We can obtain The Sixteen Basic Guarantees to Parents. Fun Disruptor Chapter Seventeen. The American people love this. They know what it means. They live it, *with quiet heartsickness and quiet desperation.* They *know.*

America's ghastly, failing, No-Mandatory-School-Homework-Schools, cause snickering in South Korea, Taiwan, Hong Kong, Singapore. It is the way we in America would respond if American high school sports teams got to play teams from a nation that did not have mandatory sports practices. It would be so easy to beat them by 70 points a game. We would be *snickering at the hapless silliness of No-Mandatory-Practice sports teams.*

We as Americans would be thinking, How dumb can people be??

California, formerly with the best schools in the world, now leads the world in Being Laughed At. California's public schools have developed, under Governor Brown's historically unique leadership, a lollipop solution to the problem of teaching algebra: drop the teaching of algebra. Brilliant! The grim denial of a prosperous future for middle-middle, lower-middle class and poor Black, Hispanic and white families continues apace.

Thanks, teachers unions. And Governor Nincompoop.

The School Professors Guild

Suuuper!Party! will, overnight, create the School Professors Guild, a new teachers union with a cute, bump-up name. (To be called a School Professor the teacher must have a Masters Degree in the subject that they teach).

Why a new teachers union? Because the current teachers unions are too deeply enmeshed in generations of sociological gobbledygook, in generations of psychobabble, and in the feckless, limp, "Inspiring the children to learn" fantasy, a fantasy that, for starters, excludes boys. These hapless unions will willingly go down to defeat and disaster in the coming Quad Co-ordinated Lawsuits, rather than change and learn, for example, from teaching in South Korea, Taiwan, Hong Kong, Singapore.

They are hopelessly intellectually incurious. They fear the word rigor. Like all long-time powers, they are pigheaded arrogant. They regard U.S. history and the U.S. Constitution as regrettable. They are lost and floundering.

Well, now they are going to *be* in the history books, under the heading, the wreckers of a prosperous future for Black America every school night, the wreckers of a prosperous future for Hispanic America every school night, the wreckers of a prosperous future for Blue collar and Pink collar America every school night, and the wreckers of a prosperous future for much of White suburban America every school night. At least they will be famous!

As the historian noted, "A people see their disaster before them, but they go into it anyway."

The School Professors Guild teachers union has already agreed to full support of all 16 points of The Sixteen Basic Guarantees to Parents. Fun Disruptor Chapter Seventeen. They told us, *"No problem at all. It is to our huge advantage as teachers."* So what do they know?

No problem at all. Words to live by.

The teachers unions and educrats have destroyed millions of Black and other families, as seen in 2,000,000 men in prison, and six million more having been in prison. Ex cons. Tens of millions of other families have been severely limited in income and social status. The gutting of Black America.

They are unlimited only in their quiet despair.

Black leaders have all been grotesquely cheated all of their adult lives by the white progressive fear and loathing

of the word rigor, just ordinary, everyday rigor. We can speculate that had Rev. Jesse Jackson discovered Mandatory School
Homework Schooling forty years ago, discovered Mandatory
School Homework the way chainsaw Korean-Americans (that's
a compliment) mean Mandatory School Homework, Rev. Jackson would have become the first Black President of the United
States, two triumphant terms, and now be an honored states-
man, worldwide. As it is, Rev. Jackson's face often looks rav-
aged, due to the above No-Mandatory-School-Homework
Catastrophes seen and suffered throughout Black America,
decade after decade, tomorrow after tormorrow.

Women as a Social Group, including women in Congress
and in the 50 state legislatures, have been and remain limited
in getting power in every sphere by the girly poetry and The
War Against Boys, of "inspiring the children to learn", and the
even more self-enfeebled, "sparking an interest". So the son of
two watchful, suspicious, ambitious, aggressive professionals
has his interest "sparked" in chemistry. What about the other
99% of the kids? *Bored slackers all.*
The choice is, Mandatory School Homework Schools.
Or, a sea of disasters.
Voters would like to choose one.

Two other sad phrases in U.S. education are,"No Child
Left Behind" and the seriously creepy, "Race to the Top".
In both instances, these ghastly fantasies mean, "But without
Mandatory School Homework Schools". So sad. So pathetic. So
artless. So intellectually immature. Malfeasance. Criminal theft
of public monies.

The only way to inspire the small percentage of children who
do ever become "inspired" is by Mandatory School Homework
Schools. Many straight 'A' Asian-American boys and Jewish-
American boys graduate from grade twelve with Honors, and

completely uninspired. Bored, alienated, cynical, smirking. So what do they do? They shrug, and go off to Harvard and M.I.T. and Stanford.

All 535 Members of Congress are Victimized

Another social group that is victimized by the current cultural regime that holds the goofy-poop ideology that "success in grade school education is about inspiring the children to learn" is all 535 members of Congress themselves. Congress victimized? Powerful Congressmen and Congresswomen victims? Yes. BECAUSE it is not humanly possible to raise up lower middle class and poor and middle-middle income people into the upper middle class without actually-mandatory, Mandatory School Homework Schools.

Both Progressives and Conservatives are equally hobbled. It is like the Dems and the Reps are condemned to a perpetual three-legged race, with each other. Yikes! Talk about misery!

Congress is severely handicapped, hobbled by this failed culture. For each member of Congress, *Progressives and Conservatives both*, it is like driving a Mercedes-Benz that has a 10 horsepower engine.

Currently, members of Congress who seek egalitarianism for disadvantaged social groups are engaged in **a totally futile endeavor**. A waste of Congressional careers, a waste of their professional lives.

Senator Elizabeth Warren wants to raise the minimum wage to $22.00 an hour, the wage that she undoubtedly pays to her maid and gardener and secretarial help, $880.00 a week for each, $1,760.00 for two, plus overtime, totaling, with health care, over $100,000.00 a year. Warren's Senate salary is $174,000.00. The Senator is a generous employer. In all probability, in selfless sacrifice, she lives in a hut and drives a motor scooter, in order to pay the help.

Senator Warren, it is easy to get lower-middle class and poor people up to $22.00 an hour. Four words to live by, Senator, Mandatory School Homework Schools. The Historic Civil Rights Act for Real Egalitarianism, with the Sixteen Basic Guarantees to Parents. End the Elizabethan Caste System of Ghastly Condescension. Stop trying to preserve Classist oink-oinkism. Say no to Harvard's pompous blindness. Harvard hates America. We shall overcome!

Senator Warren believes that she is intrinsically *More Intelligent* than lower middle class and poor Inner City and Barrio and Blue collar girls and boys. There is no evidence of this pretentious, classist belief *what-so-ever.*

Worth noting: Redistributionism is a dullard's idea, and paternalistic. Redistributionism is dim-witted, pompous people assuming that lower middle class and poor people are dim-witted. It is Pomposity Unchained.

Inner City Black girls and boys are in every way as intelligent as Sen. Warren sees herself as being.

Every Democratic-Progressive initiative and legislation for egalitarianism has *no chance whatsoever of success.* Because No-School-Homeworked victims sink into the quicksand, and often drown. Drowning *you* with them. Ever notice?

Every Republican-Conservative initiative and legislation for egalitarianism has *no chance whatsoever of success.* Because No-School-Homeworked victims sink into the quicksand, and often drown. Drowning *you* with them. Ever notice?

Every Black Congressional Caucus initiative and legislation for egalitarianism has *no chance whatsoever of success.* Because No-School-Homeworked victims sink into the quicksand, and often drown. Drowning *you* with them. Ever notice?

There is the soft despotism, the Soft Slavery, of being put onto the trajectory of going-to-prison. Hard time in prison is not soft slavery.

Every Hispanic Congressional Caucus initiative and legislation for egalitarianism has *no chance whatsoever of success*. Because No-School-Homeworked victims sink into the quicksand, and often drown. Drowning *you* with them. Ever notice?

There is the soft despotism of School-Dropout-Minimum-Wageism for Latinos and Latinas.

Every Women's Congressional Caucus initiative and legislation for egalitarianism has *no chance whatsoever of success*. Because No-School-Homeworked victims, notably boys, sink into the quicksand, and often drown. Drowning *you* with them. Ever notice? Then they become Men. Uh oh.

Congresswomen should consciously, articulately abandon the Girly-Cute-Cute, Female Ghetto, Feminine Little Idea about "inspiring the children to learn". This will help to get equal power with men. Women need to step up. Swagger it out. Don't be pleasant about catastrophe.

Nothing holds women as a social group back and holds feminism back more than the awful failure to replace the current, unmanly, failed grade school education with Mandatory School Homework Schools, the Real Egalitarianism. It is like being the boy who is the schoolyard sap and chicken. Most every boy who gets so tagged gets his swagger on, moves on, and is okay.

Attempting to raise up lower middle class and poor Black Americans and any other social group without Mandatory School Homework Schools is like attempting to cook food without heat of any kind. Uncooked food is inedible and uncivilized. So are uncooked boys inedible and uncivilized.

To escape this humiliating nightmare, let there be bipartisan passage of **The Historic Civil Rights Act for Real Egalitarianism, Year 20___** with **The Sixteen Basic Guarantees to Parents**. This Revolution Against Caste is a larger liberating revolution than 1776 and 1789 combined. Then your Mercedes-Benz that had a 10 horsepower engine suddenly has a 500 horsepower engine.

Progressive U.S. Presidents and Conservative Presidents share a common malady that brings both of them down. The defeat of the aspirations of lower-middle class and poor and middle-middle class Americans by the failed culture of No-School-Homework-Schools by the teachers unions and educrats causes these social groups to *switch parties and presidencies every eight years or so*, in a futile hope. Therefore, both Progressives and Conservatives should adopt the Revolution Against Caste, the Real Egalitarianism.

In Nationally Televised U.S. Congressional Hearings on this worst domestic crisis since 1860, Congress Members should be Confrontational, Loud, and Visibly Angry.

Congresswomen might consider saying, "I am gd angry about this catastrophe in our nation. When I visited Singapore schools last week..." In our view, it is desirable not to engage in chuckling and giggling about this issue. Think, Stage Four Cancer is not for joking. Proceed with the Quad Co-ordinated Lawsuits. THE NATION WILL LOVE IT.

The major producers of poverty in America by far are the teachers unions. Not-educated causes poverty.

Members of Congress should grimly, pointedly unsmilingly, confront the teachers unions. The chances that the teachers unions will give up the foolish, obviously Untrue Formula that "success in grade school education is about inspiring the children to learn" is: Absolutely Zero. Here is the reason. *People always, always refuse to give up the dominant culture and Worldview to which they adhere.*

Watch with suspicion for the following attempt to Dupe Dopey Congress Members and Dupe Dumb State Legislators:

The teachers unions will simply, secretly, redefine Mandatory School Homework Schools to mean "success in grade school education is about inspiring the children to learn."

"A people see their disaster before them, but they go into it anyway." A historic train wreck is coming, like the white supremacist South refusing to see reality.

Congress members can add to their power by consciously leaving this sad, intellectually immature fantasy behind, exchanged for the power in passing **The Historic Civil Rights Act for Real Egalitarianism** with the **Sixteen Basic Guarantees for Parents**. And by **The Quad Co-ordinated Lawsuits** that will greatly delight America. Fun Disruptor Chapters Seventeen and Chapter Eighteen here.

Ask parents among your constituents what they want. This issue is hugely empowering for you, and for your constituents.

Women in Elective Public Office, Wanna Be Governor?

Wanna be President of the United States? Then become a grim fanatic about Real Egalitarianism of access by 100% of parents to Mandatory School Homework Schools at Top World Class Level, in which the parent-chosen school takes 100% of the responsibility to supervise that the school homework is done. Be serious and unsmiling, rather than cheerful and chuckling. Be known as tough and unyielding. To unnerve your foes, go with the Quad Co-ordinated Lawsuits against the teachers unions.

Adopt the normally firm, merely normal rigor of The Sixteen Basic Guarantees to Parents. Fun Disruptor Chapter Seventeen.

Don't be so "nice". Use an expletive here and there. "I am completely fed up with this word-that-rhymes-with-excrement." "This is Gd effing nonsense and you know it." Such language on national television? Yes. If you become known as a Tough Bitch, *enjoy the compliment.* Wear it as a badge of honor. As FDR said, "I wear their hatred as a Badge of Honor." Hatred of her didn't bother the ever unsmiling Margaret Thatcher, the Iron Lady.

The default expression on men is the unsmiling demeanor. 'Don't mess with me'. The default expression on women is the smile. 'I am nice, I am no threat, be nice to me'.

Try the man's default expression.

Suuuper!Party! hybrid candidates must agree not to accept any contributions under any guise, including ground game assistance, from the teachers unions.

No Contributions Accepted. Due to us obtaining, due to the U.S., obtaining the *Real Egalitarianism* by The Historic Civil Rights Act for Real Egalitarianism, Year 20__ with The Sixteen Basic Guarantees to Parents.

No Contributions Accepted. Due to the decision by Suuuper!Party! to arrange, if insulted or confronted, prosecution of these unions for Fraud, Misrepresentation, and Malfeasance with Public Funds in the wrecking of a prosperous future for Black America every school night, the wrecking of a prosperous future for Hispanic America every school night, the wrecking of a prosperous future for Blue collar and Pink collar America every school night, and the wrecking of a prosperous future for much of White suburban America every school night.

No Contributions Accepted. This issue, this crisis, this scandal and this liberation is 1,000 times more important than union intransigence. Margaret Thatcher as Prime Minister made her reputation by confronting toxic British unions that caused far, far less damage to Britain than the teachers unions have caused to America and to Black America among others.

No Contributions Accepted. Due to this scandal and national crisis that is literally and actually 1,000,000 times worse than Watergate and Enron, the teachers unions are in no position to threaten anyone who is past primary school, not in Congress nor in the 50-state legislatures, nor on Wall Street. Or the persons or party that is insulted or confronted can respond by pointedly joining and organizing the Quad Co-ordinated Lawsuits against the teachers unions and educrats.

The teachers unions and their funds stand to be placed under federal custody, with U.S. Justice Department assistant attorneys-general and F.B.I. agents permanently in-house. "Good morning, F.B.I. Special Agent Masters. My, what an early bird you are. You know, I always admire your 6-foot-9 height. I brought you coffee the way you like it."

The custody would include the pension funds, which are now misused in malfeasance for political reasons. The pension funds require Wall Street help, with Suuuper!Party! paramount in *selecting the hedge fund chief executive custodians.*

Conclusion for the teachers unions, Be nice, real nice to Congressional investigators, state-legislators, and to Wall Street.

Can't We All Just Get Along?

Just a thought, for embracing the Real Egalitarianism of access by 100% of parents, beginning at Grade One, to Mandatory School Homework Schools at top world class level, in which the parent-chosen school takes 100% of the responsibility to supervise that the school homework is done, as described herein: perhaps the noted teachers unions Board Members who actually-adopt The Historic Civil Rights Act for Real Egalitarianism, with The Sixteen Basic Guarantees to Parents, can be given, with board approval in advance, the one billion MAiN National Honor Award, as given to the 2,000 boards of the

Forbes' Global 2,000 largest corporations, plus unions. On this proposal, too, Suuuper!Party! will consult with hedge-fund chief executives, and Congress. We like Wall Street. We love Wall Street! We love hedge funds. Why should you be criticized for who you love? Fun Disruptor Chapter Five.

How should individual teachers union board members respond to this more than 1,000,000 times Watergate national crisis, scandal and malfeasance that makes Enron look like a little girl taking an extra cookie from the cookie jar?

One answer: Become a Confidential Informant, a Co-operating Witness or Unnamed Witness. Wear a wire for the U.S. Department of Justice and the F.B.I. You will be a national hero. The Persons of the Year on the cover of Time Magazine, 2002, were three women whistleblowers. Google it.

Hero Labor Union Leaders: Labor union leaders should realize that they can obtain far greater wealth for their members by the Real Egalitarianism of, The Historic Civil Rights Act for Real Egalitarianism, with The Sixteen Basic Guarantees to Parents. *This is to double the family income of union members.* All sons and daughters go to university.

Lower Middle Class and Poor Families have the Highest De facto Taxes

Consider a lower-middle class or poor family in, say, South Side Chicago, that has four school age children. In practice today, they will not finish school, especially boys. And the poverty continues. And worse, young males getting in trouble with the law, even deadly trouble, and young women getting themselves pregnant and dropping out into lives of poverty.

These young Black people have essentially nothing to do on school days from midday to midnight. Is it any wonder that boys and girls get into trouble? What could possibly go wrong with twelve hours a day of teenager idleness?

In contrast, with Mandatory School Homework Schools, beginning at grade one with unrelenting Mandatory School Homework, 200 times a year, for 12 years, sons and daughters *go to university as a matter of course.* The result: each of the four educated adults, cited in the above-noted South Side Chicago family, makes $25,000-a-year more than they otherwise would. Over ten years, this is, at $100,000-a-year total for the four, $1,000,000. It is millions of dollars over their working lifetime.

To add $25,000 a year per adult in a family is: **the Real Egalitarianism, the Real Equality**.

Thus we can say that lower-middle class or poor families are, so to speak, the highest taxed families in America.

Oh, and Mandatory School Homework is free.

In a fifteen trillion dollar annual gross national product in the U.S., **Black America would have had Two Trillion Dollars greater annual income with a normal grade school education system**.

It is a known fact worldwide, known for centuries, like the Second Law of Thermodynamics, that: There Is No Success In Grade School Education Without Mandatory School Homework, Daily Audited. The teachers unions and the U.S. Department of Education's pablum-sociology, No-Mandatory-School-Homework for Black people, Caste System and racism costs Black America two trillion dollars a year in income.

The results constitute a tragedy and a despotism for Black America that is beyond trillion dollar calculations.

Teachers unions, pay up.

The tragedy and destruction is seen as well in lower middle class Hispanic families and in Blue Collar and Pink Collar families, and in middle-middle America. Hispanic parents receive a letter from their son's school, "Your son has been absent for the past *150 days* of school." This is a school *system*? What is the system? It is chaos.

Thus it is that we have an American scandal that is one million times worse than that teeny tiny Watergate scandal or than the itsy-bitsy little Enron scandal or than the 2008 Wall Street scandals, or any other scandal that can be named since 1860.

Black and Latino leaders and Democratic National Committee and Republican National Committee spokespersons and White House candidates should weigh-in relentlessly, daily, on the wrecking of a prosperous future for Black America every school night, the wrecking of a prosperous future for Hispanic America every school night, the wrecking of a prosperous future for Blue collar and Pink collar America every school night, and the wrecking of a prosperous future for much of White suburban America every school night. Needed is the Real Egalitarianism, with the most important Civil Rights Legislation in generations.

For tens of millions of struggling families the Real Egalitarianism means: "He's off to university, Electrical Engineering, instead of 7-11 clerk. We are so grateful."
"He's off to university, studying Nanotech, instead of bound for jail. A dream for us."
"She's off to Medical School, OB/GYN, instead of pregnant drop-out. **We're Moving Up!**"

Our Modern Dark Age

America does not have 2,000,000 men in prison. America has 2,000,000 *No-School-Homeworked-Men in prison*, plus 6,000,000 NSHM ex-cons, most of whom would not be there if they had been Mandatory School Homeworked. They would be in university or be university grads.
The percentage of men of any social group, including Black men and Hispanic men, in prison for violent crimes should be the same as the percentage of Jewish men and Asian-American

men in prison for violent crimes. The difference: Mandatory School Homework, 5 times a week, 200 times a year, for 12 years, totaling 2,400 daily-audited, Mandatory School Homework assignments.

Ninety-nine percent, or more, of the men in our prisons are No-School-Homeworked males. Mandatory School Homeworked males, maybe one percent. If that.

This is *Our Modern Dark Age*. It is a barbaric injustice. It is a loathsome paternalism. It is a foul racism worse than whatever the KKK now practices. The Teachers Unions cause 1,000 times the damage each year to the American Black community than does the KKK. Or, 10,000 times.

This Dark Crime must be stopped. This Modern Slavery of Black Men Made Helpless must be stopped now. The solution is free. Emancipation is free.

Before 1860, it was against the law to teach Black people how to read. Evidently the teachers unions believe that law is still on the books.

The crime rate among Black males and Hispanic males and lower middle class and poor white males can be reduced to the crime rate among Asian-American males and Jewish males. That is, Not Mandatory School Homeworked versus Mandatory School Homeworked. The latter simply make different life choices. A world of difference.

Black leaders can then say, "Free at last, free at last." Every Black leader should be able to look at his or her watch at eight o'clock each school evening and say, "Every Black boy and girl is doing hours of school homework that he or she does not want to do, intends to avoid, intends to evade, but is *required* to do to avoid being held in detention after school tomorrow. And each Black young man and woman is going to go to university to study difficult disciplines." Liberated at last!

For Social Group Leaders and Legislators, the Great Rule of Life is: They who are compelled to do the most school homework, WIN. They go UP.

Members of Congress should hold nationally televised U.S. Congressional Hearings on this immense national crisis and scandal that makes Watergate and Enron look like jaywalking in a counry town. The Nationally televised U.S. Congressional Hearings should be numbered. First... Second.... Third.... and so on.

Prison inmates and their moms should be among the witnesses seen on television at these historic Congressional Hearings.

"When my boy got 50 years I wept for weeks. He learned to read in prison". Thanks, teachers unions.

"I am serving a sixty year sentence. I can barely read and write." Thanks, teachers unions.

If television networks seem a tad slow and foot-dragging in arranging that one of them always be carrying these Historic, Nation-changing, Nation-Liberating, World-Stunning, nationally televised U.S. Congressional Hearings, to encourage greater sincerity in media executives, popular, public mention can be made of reassigning the network Owned-and-Operated station licenses to deserving parties. Result: Sincere enthusiasm!

"America needs the **Real Egalitarianism**." The Politically-Triumphant refrain from both Republican and Democratic campaigns can be the breathtaking:

"Every middle-class and poor family can double its income in this generation."

Some people can picture this or that presidential candidate, pick *yours*, saying the above sentence for month after month on the campaign trail.

Consider the honor and **'100-Year Legacy' for The Founders Of World Treasury Bank** in doubling the wealth of lower middle class and poor, and middle class families.

Also, the rate of U.S. economic growth can be increased substantially by the above 'Real Egalitarianism': some ordinary rigor in studies in parent-chosen schools.

The LOCOMOTIVE of *every* economy is: <u>Mandatory School Homework Schools</u>. Consider South Korea and Singapore, from disaster and sinkhole up to brilliantly rich at top world class level in short order. Economists should write books on the topic.

Someone should write a book, after Alfred Thayer Mahan's The Influence of Sea Power Upon History, **The Influence Of Mandatory School Homework Schools On History**. It is a thousand-page book. Greater than sea power.

Mandatory School Homework Schools also naturally inculcate in the students these qualities: Planning. Thinking ahead. Timeliness. Deferment of gratification. Studiousness. Patience. Respect for women in boys and girls. Responsibility. Decision to go to university. Ambition.

Another term for all this is, Upper Middle Class Culture.

Mandatory School Homework Schools are: <u>the sole redistributionism that works</u>.

Redistributionism of wealth never actually happens. It is lost on No School Homeworked Males in any case. <u>No School Homeworked Males</u> too often become: rogue anti-social, or willful dead enders, or criminal.

Women at Dead End

Among the many social groups that suffer from the Failed Culture of No School Homework Schools are: Women. Women suffer most. As noted above. Mandatory School Homework Schools create much better boyfriends and husbands. The usual difficulties in life, yes, the usual fool men, yes, but much alleviated by educated men with career trajectories, and incomes, and vested interest in stability at home.

The nation will be justifiably deeply angry at the biggest domestic scandal and crisis in American history since 1860, deeply bitter about the wrecking of a prosperous future for so many tens of millions of Americans.

Heroes to the American People

Legislators who confront the teachers unions and educrats will be heroes to the American people. A strike is an empty threat from the teachers unions. There are millions of early-retired professionals who can replace them, and who are not scaredy-cat of Mandatory School Homework Schools.

Suuuper!Party! offers to the Republican National Committee and candidates, and to Democratic National Committee and candidates these election winners:
The Real Egalitarianism, the Real Equality's doubling of the income of middle-middle class and lower middle class and poor Americans in one generation.
Suuuper!Party! also offers FREE UNIVERSITY FOR ALL FOREVER. This, too, offers the doubling of the income of middle-middle class and lower middle class and poor Americans in one generation. Parenthetically, it helps young women who want to get married and have children, a boost to doing so, as the couple will have no worries about paying for university education for themselves and their children.

Candidates for 500,000 Elective Public Offices

Suuuper!Party! also offers the category killer, the App of Apps, **The World Parliament Of Women**.

Suuuper!Party! also offers: Congress TV Channel, and Democratic Party TV Channel and Republican Party TV Channel. If anyone complains, tattle-tale to the Democratic National Committee, 202-863-8000, and to the Republican National Committee, 202-863-8500. For sincere revenge.

500,000 Candidates: Suuuper!Party! can, as a nation-thrilling option, invite hybrid candidates to run for all 500,000 elective public offices, from President of the United States, to all 8,000 State Legislators in the 50 states, to all School Board Officials. And sheriffs and dog catchers.

This phenomenon would be amazing and pleasing to the nation. Not without open-mouthed awe in the Beltway.

Suuuper!Party! can arrange overnight a download of 10,000 MAiN-converted-to-dollars, to 100,000,000 voters who click, "I Will Vote for the Best Suuuper!Party!-hybrid Candidate", which means to pols that their constituents have signed:

"I will vote for the de facto hybrid Republican-Suuuper!Party! candidate.

Or vote for the de facto hybrid Democratic-Suuuper!Party! candidate."

The 10,000-MAiN app download for a World Treasury Bank Savings Account, perhaps-worth-$10,000, perhaps not, plus the 10,000-MAiN perhaps-worth-$10,000 download for Suuuper!Party!, perhaps $20,000 total, if delayed, will cause much pain. Most Americans cannot put their hands on even $2,000.00.

100,000,000 Americans times 20,000 is Two Trillion MAiN. 100,000,000 to 200,000,000 Americans will not be denied.

No U.S. administration wants or can bear 100,000,000+ American voters to be insisting on the right to transfer U.S. dollars in a World Treasury Bank account to their U.S. dollar account in the USA. In such an event, the ballot box looms for any officious delays. This can gather in tens of millions of votes, and decide who wins presidential and congressional elections.

They used to be kind of sort of Anti-Semitic

It is worth noting that one of the significant causes of anti-Semitism is resentment of success, resentment in No-School-Homework social groups, not excluding Germany et al in the 1930s. Give these fools Mandatory School Homework Schools and the result is, "Your father and I really like your new boy-friend, Jason Goldberg, that you met in Stanford Computer Science." Well, that's a slight change in Mr. and Mrs. Boobhead! The reduction of fecklessness is always useful in the human race, however uncommon may be the procedure.

World Treasury Bank MAiN

Ba-a-a-ad: What World Treasury Bank wants, World Treasury Bank gets. World Treasury Bank can, and may as well, with its super pal Suuuper!Party!, arrange legislation that would preclude any would-be competitor for MAiN.

Otherwise, Suuuper!Party! is an optimistic party: limited government, limited taxes, booming prosperity, strong defense, America is a great nation. The Penny Plan, cut 1% a year for six years, to balance the budget. America second to none in importance for this century. And Century 2100 as well: Fun Disruptor Chapter Twenty-four.

And, **America with the best and most rigorous schools in the world for all social groups and classes**, a nation equipped with: the deepest, most pronounced egalitarianism in history, the *Real* Egalitarianism, the *Real* Equality, far beyond mere condescending redistributionism to *people who are being treated absolutely monstrously,* as if their sons and daughters are **Not Intelligent Enough** to do the same level of academic studies in school and university as, oh, say for example, national media television reporters did. *Middle class and lower middle class and poor Black, Hispanic and Blue Collar parents*, including the 80% to 90% of parents who are not able to be attentive to school homework being done, 200 times a year, *know this*, and realize with great relief that the Real Egalitarianism, the Real Equality, is their ticket to *Rising Up, at long last.* A formidable political combination.

Is the Real Egalitarianism The Major Advancement in History?

Consider the honor and legacy and historicity of being responsible for the Revolution Against Caste, that is, the Real Egalitarianism, which might come to be seen as, The Major Advancement In History.

Consider how this astonishing suggestion just might be true. The other great revolutions and human advancements, nevertheless left over 90% of the people half-educated or quarter-educated. For examples: 1776. 1789. The vote for women. The right of the working class to organize. Civil rights for Black people. Independence for colonized peoples. *In all cases, these events left the beneficiaries essentially helpless through lack of real education.* The immense, tragic results of this failure are still seen worldwide.

Humanity has nothing to lose but the chains of Caste System injustice.

Humanity has nothing to throw off but the chains of Caste System injustice.

The Real Egalitarianism, is, then, actually, a bigger and more important advancement for middle class and poor people worldwide than any in the past.

Or, perhaps the Revolution Against Caste is merely rather quite important. Whatever.

A thousand history books may be written over the next 1,000 years.

The Founders of World Treasury Bank MAiN will be included, with photos and video, in these books.

The above-noted offers a treasure trove of material for You-Tube and Facebook and Twitter entrants in the opportunity to apply for very large awards that might be paid out. Fun Disruptor Awards Chapter Thirty.

Fun Disruptor Chapter Nineteen

The Fourteenth of Twenty-three Currency-Validations by World Treasury Bank MAiN that Really Please Humanity.

This is How Billionaires Can Be Acclaimed Worldwide for Decades by Popular, Liberating Actions from World Treasury Bank, the MAiN, and its Founders.

THE UNIVERSITIES EMPEROR HAS NO CLOTHES

World Treasury Bank MAiN Founders can become heroes in America and beyond. Because there can be great, world-delighting, world amazing, class action lawsuits by "10,000,000" or "20,000,0000" graduates of universities.

These can be lawsuits by grads for fraud, misrepresentation, and malfeasance by the universities.

As Matthew Kaminski, a member of the Wall Street Journal Editorial Board reports in an interview with Yale university professor, Donald Kagan, April 27, 2013, "Universities, he proposed, are failing students and hurting American democracy. Curricula are 'individualized, unfocused and scattered.' On campus, he said, 'I find a kind of cultural void, an ignorance of the past, a sense of rootlessness and aimlessness.' Rare are 'faculty with atypical views,' he charged. 'Still rarer is an informed understanding of the traditions and institutions of our Western civilization and of our country and an appreciation of their special qualities and values.' He counseled schools to adopt 'a common core of studies' in the history, literature and philosophy 'of our culture.'

Similar territory was explored by Alan Bloom in his 1987, "The Closing of the American Mind."

Herewith mantras for these **'I graduated from university, but I am not an educated person'** class action lawsuits that stand to cause delighted smiles in all 50 states, and all over the world. Great fun. And great history. See if you agree:

I graduated from university. I received my university diploma from a major university. BUT I AM NOT AN EDUCATED PERSON.

I do not know any real mathematics. I can barely do simple arithmetic. I AM NOT AN EDUCATED PERSON.

I do not know any of the sciences. The Second Law of Thermodynamics is what?

I do not know any history, except History as the professors' American Anti-Americanism.

Does the United States of America have a History worth knowing? *I DO NOT KNOW.*

I do not know the History of the past 2,500 years, from Ancient Greece and Rome up to today. Which came first, Rome or Greece? Ref., The Uniqueness of Western Civilization by Professor Ricardo Duchesne. For this reason, I AM NOT AN EDUCATED PERSON.

Is Europe historically a great civilization? *I DO NOT KNOW*. Is America first rank? I DO NOT KNOW. I was never instructed at the world famous university that I attended.

What is Bastille Day? Is that a type of candy? What is Kristallnacht? Where is it? The professors: Silent. What is Iwo Jima? I HAVE NO IDEA.

I do not know any economics, except anti-free enterprise agitprop. **How does our American economy work? I have no idea.** What are Milton Friedman, Free Enterprise economics? I HAVE NO IDEA. I GRADUATED FROM UNIVERSITY BUT I AM NOT AN EDUCATED PERSON.

I have not been educated in any political science, except Leftism-Is-Truth. I AM NOT AN EDUCATED PERSON.

I do not know the Constitution of the United States. What is it about? How did it get here? Does the Constitution of our nation matter? Please tell me. I HAVE NO IDEA.

Was our American Civil War fought in the Eighteenth Century or the Seventeenth Century? I HAVE NO IDEA. I have a diploma from a prestige university on the wall, but I AM NOT AN EDUCATED PERSON.

What is the length of a U.S. Senate term? Is it four years? I HAVE NO IDEA.

What is the size of the national debt? I HAVE NO IDEA.

The universities that I and my friends attended offered virtually no courses on American political, diplomatic, military and intellectual history. There are no course offerings on Ancient Greece and Rome. The few courses offered are characterized by professorial resentment of the U.S., and disdain for the American people, for not being socialist. **I was not forewarned of these Material Facts as required by Contract Law**. I and my fellow alumni look forward to being plaintiffs in the coming, historic, Class Action Lawsuits by millions of grads.

Universities can teach whatever they want. Once again: Universities can teach absolutely whatever they want. But they must practice Full Disclosure as required by Contract Law, and Truth in Advertising. I paid $250,000.00 *for what*?? I AM NOT AN EDUCATED PERSON. WE DEMAND OUR MONEY BACK WITH TRIPLE DAMAGES.

The president of the company that I work for grimly informed me that I confuse its and it's. I cannot even write the English language properly! What percentage is 48,373 of 627,389? I don't know how to do percentages. I HAVE A UNIVERSITY DIPLOMA BUT I AM NOT AN EDUCATED PERSON. I DEMAND MY MONEY BACK!

Many course titles and descriptions are in pablum language that seeks to conceal the agenda. The language is Slither Language, and seeks to cover-up that no matter the subject, the course is composed of: Socialism-Is-Truth. The professors want to run the U.S. economy. They are nutcase ambitious, a group of Little Napoleons. We were never given Full Disclosure as required by Contract Law. I HAVE A UNIVERSITY DIPLOMA BUT I AM NOT AN EDUCATED PERSON. I DEMAND MY MONEY BACK!

Anti-Semitism is growing on many U.S. university campuses, as continuingly reported in Frontpagemag.com. Is this not an evil? MY PROFESSORS SAID NOTHING, NOT ONE WORD. Is Silence consent? The professors are anti-Israel, which fact was never disclosed to me at recruitment, as is required by Contract Law, or when I paid $250,000.00 to the university. I was not informed, as required by Contract Law, that unimpeded anti-Semitism is growing on the campus. **I and my alumni friends have all been swindled**. I HAVE A UNIVERSITY DIPLOMA BUT I AM NOT AN EDUCATED PERSON. I DEMAND MY MONEY BACK PLUS TRIPLE DAMAGES! The universities accept federal and state money. They can be sued for malfeasance under federal racketeering laws.

I know nothing of the religions, except anti-Christian animus and anti-Israel anger that little conceals growing anti-Semitism on university campuses, *and little conceals the professors' romance with totalitarian despotisms and their crimes and horrors*. Ref. One Party Classroom, and, Indoctrination U, and, The Heterodoxy Handbook, and, Reforming Our Universities, all by David Horowitz. I GRADUATED FROM UNIVERSITY BUT I AM NOT AN EDUCATED PERSON.

Do the world's 2.3 Billion Protestants and Catholics, equal to the population of China and India *combined*, count for *nothing*? Zero? India plus China equal *Nothing??* I was not forewarned of these Material Facts as required by Contract Law. Our Intellectually Immature, Provincial Boob Professors said nothing, not one word. Newsmax.com and David Horowitz's Frontpagemag.com report that 200 million Christians in the world are persecuted and oppressed, equal to two-thirds the population of the U.S. Why weren't we told by the damn fool, eyes-closed, ignorant professors? I HAVE A UNIVERSITY DIPLOMA BUT I AM NOT AN EDUCATED PERSON! I DEMAND MY MONEY BACK, PLUS TRIPLE DAMAGES!

Multiculturalism is not a culture. Multiculturalism is the lack of a culture. If all Civilizations and Nations and Cultures and Oil Paintings and Novels and Motion Pictures are to be considered equal, fine, but *under Contract Law, it was required that I be informed in advance that this is the university's worldview.*

I could have saved \$250,000.00 and five years of my life.

Suspending all judgment is a sign of education and intellect? Isn't it the reverse?? *The purpose of having a brain is to draw distinctions.* British columnist Melanie Phillips notes, "the refusal to transmit a common culture through education, the Balkanization of Britain through multiculturalism....." If this is the view of the Dull-witted Professors, fine, but they were obligated, under Contract Law, to inform us in advance, before I paid a quarter-of-a-million dollars to these Ponzi-Scheme Professors. The professors are Multi-Cultural Mambo Dancers. But, People of Intellect? No. Is there an American culture? What is American culture? I am an American. If this means nothing in the view of the professors, fine, but they are obligated, under Contract Law, to inform us in advance of their resentment against America. **This System is the Long Con by the professors and universities**. I HAVE A UNIVERSITY DIPLOMA BUT I AM NOT AN EDUCATED PERSON! I DEMAND MY MONEY BACK, PLUS TRIPLE DAMAGES!

The universities swindled, duped, and humiliated all of my fellow alumni, and current students, more than 20,000,000 people total. I HAVE A UNIVERSITY DIPLOMA BUT I AM NOT AN EDUCATED PERSON! I DEMAND MY MONEY BACK, PLUS TRIPLE DAMAGES! I will join the class action lawsuits by 10,000,000, perhaps 20,000,000 and more plaintiffs. Enough, enough and more than enough of the universities' Gigantic Farce of Ignorance.

Was Winston Churchill a major historical figure? Reportedly, thirty percent of British young people think that Winston Churchill is a fictional figure. Is he? Or was he real? *I DO NOT KNOW.*

What is the Cold War? Was that major history? Who was at war? What was the war about? Who won? Or is the Cold War about the climate? I HAVE NO IDEA. I GRADUATED MAGNA CUM LAUDE FROM A MAJOR, PRESTIGIOUS UNIVERSITY BUT I AM NOT AN EDUCATED PERSON. I DEMAND MY MONEY BACK. I await the historic, class action lawsuits. We must get triple-damages.

When was World War I fought? Many British people think World War I was fought in the 17th Century. Was it? Was it maybe the 16th Century? Who was at war? What was the war about? I HAVE NO IDEA. I AM UNIVERSITY "EDUCATED" BUT I AM NOT AN EDUCATED PERSON.

Are human beings meaningless blobs of protoplasm? The professors believe that, **Human Beings Are Meaningless**, but failed to fully disclose this fact in advance, as required by Contract Law. I have no idea whether Human Beings are Meaningless. There is no university intellectual inquiry about Meaning. This *is* meaninglessness. I GRADUATED FROM UNIVERSITY, BUT I AM NOT AN EDUCATED PERSON.

I paid $250,000.00 to be taught that America is an Imperial, Malignant and Loathsome power. And that America is a Stupid and Accidental Power. The professors believe this. That is their right. But they failed to fully disclose this material fact in advance, as required by Contract Law. I DEMAND MY $250,000.00 BACK, WITH TRIPLE DAMAGES!

Who was Joseph Stalin? What did he do? Was he a poet? I HAVE NO IDEA.
Who was Mahatma Gandhi? Was he a clothing designer? I HAVE NO IDEA.

I do not know any Shakespeare, the world's greatest writer by far. I HAVE A UNIVERSITY DIPLOMA BUT I AM NOT AN EDUCATED PERSON! I DEMAND MY MONEY BACK, PLUS TRIPLE DAMAGES!

I do not know any real sociology except that, A Man is a Woman with a penis. You think?
A Boy is: a Girl with a penis. Really?

I do not know any psychology except psycho-babble and psycho-pablum.

How come professors hardly work at all, and are often silly frivolous? I paid a fortune for Gravitas and Learning. I was typically taught by bored, sullen, socialist, scruffy, grad students who were galley slaves paid so little that they qualified for welfare assistance, while the lazy professors and lord-high, maharajah administrators glom high six-figure and seven-figure salaries, salaries paid by us Pathetic, Sucker, Students. For what?? I GRADUATED FROM UNIVERSITY BUT I AM NOT AN EDUCATED PERSON. I DEMAND BY MONEY BACK! There was never Full Disclosure to me by the university, as required by Contract Law.

I DEMAND MY MONEY BACK! PLUS TRIPLE DAMAGES!

These class action lawsuits are intrinsically for $500,000,000,000 (Five hundred billion dollars). This would be only 10,000,000 Angry, Cheated, Suckered, Swindled graduates suing for only $50,000 each. There may well be a multiple of ten million plaintiffs. The case can be made that these are lawsuits for more than One Trillion Dollars.

U.S. states should sue their own state university administrators and professors, for Fraud, Misrepresentation, and

Malfeasance with Public Funds, and launch Equal Employment Opportunity Commission lawsuits for illegal exclusions in Hiring. And Promotion. And Tenure.

The U.S. itself should sue universities that are recipients of government billions and hundreds of billions of dollars, lawsuits for fraud, misrepresentation, and malfeasance. Also, wire fraud.

Expect sales of spirits to spike where professors and university administrators buy their liquor. Vodka may be going out the door by the case.

Would these lawsuits affect universities of top, world class reputation, such as Harvard, Yale, all Ivy League universities, Stanford and so on? Certainly. The only way that a student in the humanities at Harvard can graduate without 'Honors' is to spit in the punchbowl at the professor's party. Ninety-one per cent get Honors, and grads still cannot write paragraphs in the English language. Sociological gobbledygook, psycho-babble and socialist cant, yes. English, no.

Better not hire the 9% who ingloriously fail to graduate from Harvard with honors. They might drool a bit.

The Universities Emperor Has No Clothes Equals Enormous Fun

These history-making, Great Fun, Huge Enjoyment, class action lawsuits, that will bring smiles to the nation, and to the world, can easily be put together, including by full-page ads in major newspapers, and by a consortium of major law firms.

These Extremely Rude and Cheerfully So Very Disrespectful lawsuits stand to be covered by an awestruck world media, and be enjoyed by hundreds of millions of people worldwide. *THE WHOLE NATION WILL BE ELATED!* People will be laughing with pleasure and high-fiving in bars and restaurants.

What does the word Schadenfreude mean?

This *huge fun and fabulous enjoyment by a delighted nation* can be launched as World Treasury Bank MAiN is put together. Let major law firms make themselves known. No, you are not going to get forty per cent. Sorry! The first thing we do, let's kill all the lawyers. Whatever.

Suuuper!Party! and its presidential candidate and other candidates will support and advance these lawsuits, including lawsuits by the U.S. and state legislatures regarding malfeasance with public funds. Let there be a historic series of nationally televised U.S. Congressional Hearings.

Suuuper!Party! also supports that the U.S. and the 50 state legislatures, and these Historic Congressional Hearings, should require of each university that receives public monies to produce Five Documents, each year, that must be included, as Full Disclosure, in their student recruitment book.
And: in any application for Public Funds.

DOCUMENT ONE: A list of What An Educated Person Should Know. In the university's view. For the third time in this book, **Universities can teach absolutely whatever they want**

DOCUMENT TWO: Full Disclosure of What Is Included in The University's Own Core Curriculum, including with reference to each of the issues included in Fun Disruptor Chapter Nineteen herein.

DOCUMENT THREE: Referencing Business Insider, June 14, 2013, "Colleges Have Botched the Way They Handle Rape On Campus, with fraternity "rape factories" and '19% of undergraduate women reporting experiencing attempted or completed sexual assault'.'" Document Three requires that each university list its policies regarding reported rapes, and, invite victims of rape at the college to come forward publicly.

DOCUMENT FOUR: Whether there is anti-Semitism on the campus. This is not referring to the unknowable that is inner thoughts. This refers to campus anti-Semitic events as covered in the daily articles in David Horowitz's, Frontpagemag.com's five weekly emails of compelling articles. Free. Great.

DOCUMENT FIVE: The university's auditable policies and practices in Hiring, Promotion, and, Tenure. The profs love Inclusiveness and Tolerance. They are learned men and women. Hello! Intellectual variety fascinates them no end.

Legislators should insist, each year, on meeting the newly promoted and tenured professors. To enjoy intellectual variety. Oh, and to uncover continuing fraud and malfeasance with public funds, and you legislators being Duped-as-Dopes, as Big Saps, Big Time.

Let a bi-partisan, large group of Congress members proceed now with a series of numbered, nationally televised U.S. Congressional Hearings. The fifty state legislatures can do the same in their state. Require that the university's student recruitment book, with Full Disclosures as noted herein, and, the above-noted Five Documents, be shown, each year, to legislators *Before New Money Can Be Appropriated for the University.*

Pour encourager les autres!

These history-making lawsuits will make heroes, indeed historic heroes, noted in history book written decades from now, out of the Major Players who come together as Founders of World Treasury Bank MAiN. This is a small part of *How Billionaires Became Popular.*

The Makers of a New Enlightenment.

The above-noted offers a treasure trove of material for You-Tube and Facebook and Twitter entrants in the opportunity to apply for very large awards that might be paid out. Fun Disruptor Awards Chapter Thirty.

Fun Disruptor Chapter Twenty

The Fifteenth of Twenty-three Currency-Validations by World Treasury Bank MAiN that Really Please Humanity.

This is How Billionaires Can Be Acclaimed Worldwide for Decades by Popular, Liberating Actions from World Treasury Bank, the MAiN, and its Founders.

THAT WORLD TREASURY BANK MAY BE AS POWERFUL AS A MAJOR NATION

World Treasury Bank can offer up to 100,000 **Perpetual Seat Trusts**, of 100,000,000 MAiN each, to the parliamentary and congressional legislatures in 150+ nations, that pass an Enabling Act, to accept the Seat Trusts. The Parliamentary and Congressional Seat Trusts' income would be for "Good Works and Personal Expenditures" by each legislator. As judged solely by his or her constituents.

The above ten trillion total is doable among a World Treasury Bank worldwide issuance. The legislators would not be the trustees.

Seat Trusts can be given and received as **National Honor Awards**, for embracing the Real Egalitarianism, for effecting, The Historic Civil Rights Act for Real Egalitarianism, Year 20___, which, shattering the age-old Caste System in education, may be seen by some as the Major Advancement for the Human

Race in the Past 5,000 years. Or at least really rather important. Fun Disruptor Chapter Eighteen.

Each Seat Trust might pay out some millions of MAiN per year to the legislator, perhaps worth some millions of dollars or Euros a year, for Good Works and Personal Expenditures.

Any individual member of Congress or Parliament can hold a news conference to announce that he or she intends to accept their seat's National Honor Award Perpetual Seat Trust for, "Good Works and Personal Expenditures, and to give to the world the economic advantage of an online global currency, while continuing to fully honor our own currency."

There may be innumerable, earnest, furrowed-brow discussions on TV worldwide about seat trusts. Nevertheless, the Plan is irresistible. Because: *Members of parliaments and congress members worldwide are completely fed-up with having only bureaucratic salaries.* In the U.S., many top level, Maharajah Bureaucrats glom over $200,000 a year, more than the mere, Lunkhead, Lower, Lesser, U.S. Senators and more than Mere Punk-ass U.S. Representatives.

The Lords of Bureaucracy stay in the Presidential Suite at 5-Star hotels, looking down.... from the heights....

This disempowerment really rankles all 535 Members of Congress. They are storing this up under the heading, "Someday, we will put them in their place."

Good news, someday is here.

The more controversy and television discussions about Perpetual Seat Trusts, the better. The Perpetual Seat Trusts Plan will be called bold, and brazen. This is a problem? As Facebook Founder and Chief Executive Mark Zuckerberg puts it, "Move fast and break things."

Congress Loves World Treasury Bank
Why Parliaments Love World Treasury Bank

A prediction: The Members of Parliament and Congress in 150+ nations will quietly be deciding to publicly accept their Seat Trust. Perhaps their spouses might helpfully help them to make this helpful decision.

People get used to changed landscapes. What seemed to be startling, becomes normal.

A Congress Member's and Parliamentary Member's constituents are the sole judge of whether his or her Good Works, and, Personal expenditures, are appropriate. Most constituents will expect and require some serious probity. There may be exceptions. There is always the legislator who is seen on video crashing a $400,000 red Ferrari into a light pole at 2:00 AM. His mistress hops out of the car, so blind drunk that she upchucks on the sidewalk. Maybe *his* constituents say, "Oh, we love him anyway. We know that he has his faults but he's a good guy in general." Lucky, too, in his constituents.

Any business person can be proud to be associated with World Treasury Bank, to be a pre-eminent world institution. To be **The Greatest Bank In History**.

At Currency issuance: there can be The World Issuance Ceremony, world-telecast, on Tiananmen Square, Beijing, or wherever it is, with perhaps thousands of business leaders, and celebrities. See the Annual Convening of World Leaders, Fun Disruptor Chapter Twenty-seven.

People might say, "Better to be on the World Treasury Bank Board of Directors than be Prime Minister or President of many a nation."

Thus speaketh Google Executive Chairman Eric Schmidt, "The adult way to run a business is to run it more like a country." – Wall Street Journal, December 5, 2012.

World Treasury Bank will have a large and powerful Compliance program, at the Directors level.

Ordinary Fortune 500 lobbying and AFL-CIO lobbying is to supporting the Seat Trusts what itsy-bitsy-teeny-weeny toy cars for tots are to Daytona 500 cars. It behooves corporations and unions and others that lobby to support the Perpetual Seat Trusts for each Congressional Seat. If you like power.

The above-noted offers a treasure trove of material for You-Tube and Facebook and Twitter entrants in the opportunity to apply for very large awards that might be paid out. Fun Disruptor Awards Chapter Thirty.

Fun Disruptor
Chapter Twenty-one

The Sixteenth of Twenty-three Currency-Validations by World Treasury Bank MAiN that Really Please Humanity.

This is How Billionaires Can Be Acclaimed Worldwide for Decades by Popular, Liberating Actions from World Treasury Bank, the MAiN, and its Founders.

WHAT THE 'MAN IN THE STREET' MAY SAY ABOUT THE PLAN

HE SAYS:
"Hey, did you hear about the Planned New Currency? It's Private-Sector.

"It's called the MAiN. It's worldwide. A bunch of Big Financial Types are bringing it in.

"Best of all, World Treasury Bank is going to validate the currency by letting TWO BILLION people download 10,000 MAiN each for *free* to your smartphone.
"You get an automatic WORLD TREASURY BANK Online Savings Account."

SHE SAYS:
"What good is it, though? I don't understand."

HE SAYS:
"It's a Free-Market Currency.

"Want to buy an Ultrabook online from Hong Kong? Maybe it will cost 1,000 MAiN. Or buy stuff in U.S. dollars by converting MAiN to the dollar on your iPhone. You are home free."

SHE SAYS:
"I'm going to get mine."

Two Plans for World Treasury Bank loaning out money

PLAN ONE: The MAiN currency may be loaned to 10,000+ accepting banks, the nation's treasury accepting, worldwide at, say, 3%, to be in turn loaned out at a larger percent.

Loans would be solely in the home-nation currency. That is, *there is no attempt to ask sellers of goods and services, or borrowers, to accept another currency, the MAiN.*

Sellers may start offering prices in MAiN on online sites, to encourage sales worldwide. Herein may be worldwide *demand* for MAiN, increasing its value. The perhaps 2,000,000,000-plus World Treasury Bank Savings Account Holders want to have their World Treasury Bank MAiN Savings Account as well as their World Treasury Bank Home-Currency Account.

PLAN TWO: Perhaps better, there may be twice or more profit for World Treasury Bank to bring in experienced loan officers directly, to loan out money directly to borrowers at, say, 6%, rather than 3% to banks. Fun Disruptor Chapter Nine.

The above-noted offers a treasure trove of material for You-Tube and Facebook and Twitter entrants in the opportunity to apply for very large awards that might be paid out. Fun Disruptor Awards Chapter Thirty.

Fun Disruptor
Chapter Twenty-two

The Seventeenth of Twenty-three Currency-Validations by World Treasury Bank MAiN that Really Please Humanity.

This is How Billionaires Can Be Acclaimed Worldwide for Decades by Popular, Liberating Actions from World Treasury Bank, the MAiN, and its Founders.

To further validate the World Currency, in a world-stunning way:

While at the creation of the first World Currency, the MAiN, World Treasury Bank and the MAiN can found, with major investment banks:

WORLD TREASURY BANK GLOBAL STOCK EXCHANGE

The issuing corporations, which might include major media corporations, would receive Founder's stock, and their Boards of Directors, as covered in board resolutions and S.E.C. Filings, would receive Founder's stock in the World Treasury Bank Global Stock Exchange.

The World Treasury Bank Global Stock Exchange may be based in Los Angeles or New York, or in Miami for tax reasons, yet with offices in a number of nations. Offices may be the U.S. Canada. Various European Union nations. Brazil. China: Shanghai, Hong Kong. Russia. India. Israel. Australia. Singapore. Johannesburg. Liberia. Mexico.

The World Treasury Bank Global Stock Exchange may try to issue not less than one IPO per business day. Or a couple of IPOs per week, *if* quality businesses are there.

The World Treasury Bank Global Stock Exchange will try to issue not less than one IPO per five weeks from **each of five continents**.

The World Treasury Bank Global Stock Exchange would try to issue not less than one IPO per year that are led by persons from various social groups that are seldom if ever involved in IPOs. Specifically:

Black Americans. Black Africans. Latin American Indigenous. Chinese peasants. Muslim women worldwide. Women of India. Black African women. U.S.-Canada-British-Australian-New Zealand women jointly. Latin American women. Indigenous peoples. Indian Dalit (Untouchables). Sudanese Christians. Russian women.

The above-noted offers a treasure trove of material for YouTube and Facebook and Twitter entrants in the opportunity to apply for very large awards that might be paid out. Fun Disruptor Awards Chapter Thirty.

Chapter Twenty-three

The Eighteenth of Twenty-three Currency-Validations by World Treasury Bank MAiN that Really Please Humanity.

This is How Billionaires Can Be Acclaimed Worldwide for Decades by Popular, Liberating Actions from World Treasury Bank, the MAiN, and its Founders.

WORLD TREASURY BANK MAiN ACCEPTS THE CHALLENGE TO RAISE TWO, BILLION DOLLAR PRIZES FOR MEDICAL ADVANCEMENT

World Treasury Bank Accepts the Idea by Andy Kessler

Really, really smart guy Andy Kessler proposes an idea that World Treasury Bank MAiN adopts. Mr. Kessler is the author of *Eat People: And Other Unapologetic Rules for Game-Changing Entrepreneurs.*

Mr. Kessler's proposal, that we embrace, was presented in a Wall Street Journal column titled, Want to Change the World? How About a Billion Dollar Prize.

Herewith, Andy Kessler in the really, really smart, Wall Street Journal, March 13, 2013, "Last month 11 scientists were awarded $3 million each as winners of the first annual Breakthrough Prize in Life Sciences. The awards – funded by Google's Sergey Brin and his wife, Anne Wojcicki, Facebook's Mark Zuckerberg and his wife Priscilla Chan, and Russian investor Yuri Milner – are intended to recognize "excellence in research aimed at curing intractable diseases and extending human life" and to "enhance medical innovation."

"This type of prize is commendable, its generosity admirable. But it prompts a question: Will such a prize actually spur innovation or do anything to help society? Or will it be like those given to MacArthur Fellows, who receive $500,000 over five years? Last year the MacArthur winners included a marine ecologist and a stringed-instrument bow maker – in other words, those that are good at giving TED talks. Good for the winners, good for those giving out the money. For the rest of us? Not so much. But what do you expect from a prize without a contest? Human psyche gets rewarded via vanity (read Nobel, Oscars). Yet economies and entrepreneurs need the incentives of a good old-fashioned contest."

Mr. Kessler offers two specific suggestions for *one billion dollar awards each*. One, to stop or cure Alzheimers. Two, to allow spinal cords to grow, to end the awful suffering of injured spinal cord victims worldwide, persons in a wheelchair or bedridden helpless. The victims include children injured in auto accidents and other accidents worldwide.

Full and entire credit goes to Andy Kessler for his idea of billion dollar prizes, and for the two selections here.

World Treasury Bank MAiN accepts the challenge to raise the billion dollar prizes for each of these two worthy causes, via convening foundations to a convention in Las Vegas.

For legal reasons, this cannot be a promise. It is merely an intention.

The above-noted offers a treasure trove of material for You-Tube and Facebook and Twitter entrants in the opportunity to apply for very large awards that might be paid out. Fun Disruptor Awards Chapter Thirty.

Fun Disruptor
Chapter Twenty-four

The Nineteenth of Twenty-three Currency-Validations by World Treasury Bank MAiN that Really Please Humanity.

This is How Billionaires Can Be Acclaimed Worldwide for Decades by Popular, Liberating Actions from World Treasury Bank, the MAiN, and its Founders.

A MODEST LITTLE PROPOSAL

Founding Fathers II And The Founding Women

This is a Modest Proposal that we thought just to throw into the mix.

The Modest Little Proposal (MLP) is that the United States of America and Canada and Great Britain and Ireland and Australia and New Zealand and Puerto Rico and Liberia and Singapore, perhaps Iceland and Greenland, federate in a 75-state UACBAS.

Each nation keeps its parliament and parliamentary elections unchanged, as intermediary institutions, plus its Olympics teams, flag, anthem, and so on.

The Prime Ministers would be *more* powerful than before, as major figures on the world stage, as major players in the world's anchor nation, in the world's most important nation.

The Parliaments in London, Ottawa, Canberra, Wellington, Monrovia in Liberia, Ireland, Singapore, San Juan, *all
unchanged.* Except more brilliant. And more powerful.

In federation, each nation would be *more* powerful and
more independent than before federation, a bigger presence
on the world stage. Each nation's name would unto itself sig-
nify: the 75-state United America Canada Britain AustraliaNZ
States. 'Our gang is bigger than your gang.' Each citizen's vote
would mean: the globe-circling nation.

A guy says, "I'm from Ireland," or "I'm from New Zealand."
The response, "You guys rule the world."

The Irish and New Zealanders say to each other, "We are
The SuperPower." *We.* The UACBAS.

A President of the United States would ordinarily choose
to have each Prime Minister at his or her Cabinet meetings as
'Executive National Advisors'. More power for the Prime Ministers. *Much* more. More power for the President.

Consider the advantages of forming a 75-state United America Canada Britain AustraliaNZ States. The UACBAS.

The advantages in the UACBAS are *national freedom*
and *national, global power, and security.* And, greater
individual freedom and *individual power.* Greater in building a business, in travel, the freedom casually go to university across oceans, the freedom casually to relocate across
oceans, and so on. "I'm moving to California/London/Syd-
ney next month."

There would be a 150-member U.S. Senate, and a larger
House of Representatives, in Washington, D.C. The nations
would elect U.S. Senate and House members to the most powerful governing body, in the world's most important nation.
Most important by far. Quite thrilling for all.

The U.S. Constitution and Bill of Rights for the whole UACBAS. People love the U.S. freedoms of the superior Constitution ever. Socialists may pout. Pouting is cute.

Each nation would fly its traditional flag along with the flag of **The Greatest Nation That There Can Ever Be**. The updated flag would be designed with the help of design contests, and include historical elements of the old.

To speculate, the new flag could include: 13 of some icon on the flag. For the 13 Colonies. These 13 little colonies in the wilderness grew to the USA. This is, *History's Greatest Saga*. Also on the flag: The Union Jack, now on the British, Australian and New Zealand flags. The number of states, perhaps a Roman numeral on the flag. Seventy-five stars may be too many. Perhaps a solid green map of the globe-girdling nation superimposed on the flag.

Each Citizen Much Better Off

Whatever are the reasons that each Australian citizen would offer that Australia is better as one nation rather than seven separate nations;

That each New Zealander would offer that New Zealand is better off as one nation rather than two separate nations;

That each Canadian would offer that Canada is better off as one nation rather than ten separate nations with border guards;

That each American would offer that America is better off as one nation rather than fifty separate nations with fifty separate borders with border guards;

That each Brit would offer that Great Britain is better off as one nation rather than three separate nations;

And that each European would offer that European Union is better off as one union rather than twenty-seven separate nations with borders and border guards;

Are the same reasons why the United America Canada Britain AustraliaNZ States is much greater than the sum of its parts. Its citizens would have *enabled themselves* to be much better able to pursue their dreams and happiness.

The United America Canada Britain AustraliaNZ States would be **The Greatest Nation on Earth**, and, The Greatest Civilization on Earth.

Each nation's military service would remain discrete and distinct. Each has special talents. Each is typically air-land-sea integrated. Each military would take a seat on the Joint Chiefs of Staff. Sometimes the British guy would be the Chairman of the Joint Chiefs of Staff. *"Ten-hut, lowly Colonials!"* Uh oh, on second thought, maybe cancel this whole plan.

All schools in the nation would have English as the mandatory language of instruction in most every class. French taught in Quebec, Spanish in Puerto Rico.

Great Britain would be three states, England, Scotland, Wales. Overall parliamentary elections continue unchanged.

England would be the most populous of the about 75 states in the UACBAS, with its population being equal to California (the current largest delegation in Congress) plus New York State *combined*. This would be a massive Congressional Delegation for the British Bulldog. A lot of power. Brits are master parliamentarians and would succeed fabulously well in a United America Canada Britain AustraliaNZ States. It is possible that some American members of Congress may hide under their desks on the floor of the House, nervously whispering, "The British are coming, the British are coming."

Britain and Ireland can caucus together in Congress as they see fit. Even ten times a day. The two Irish legislatures now are the Northern Ireland Assembly, and, the Parliament of Ireland, called "two mutually interdependent" institutions. There is a North/South Ministerial Council.

In the UACBAS, both Northern Ireland and the Republic of Ireland would separately elect a number of Representatives to the House of Representatives in Washington, D.C., yet, together elect two All-Ireland Senators to the UACBAS Senate. If this works.

Ireland would be, with Great Britain, together in one nation, the United America Canada Britain AustraliaNZ States, a win-win situation.

Liberia would need to agree to federal supervision of grade school education for a generation or two, meaning, Real Egalitarianism of access by 100% of parents to Mandatory School Homework Schools, at Top World Class Level, The Historic Civil Rights Act for Real Egalitarianism, and the Sixteen Basic Guarantees to Parents. *Every Liberian grad would be able to go to a top university.* English is the current language of Liberia.

There would of course be one currency, the dollar. Yet, the British Federal Reserve Bank, in the UACBAS, can distribute that same currency, and it can be called the pound. Winston Churchill and Lord Nelson et al on the notes, and perhaps David Beckham, OBE and Her Ladyship Posh Spice. Same thing with Canadian and Australian and New Zealand heroes on the notes issued in these nations, and useable anywhere in the nation.

Federal taxes would be harmonized step-by-step over ten years. People like lower taxes. Health insurance, many private, consumer options, to great relief.

The Royals, just end the bowing and curtseying, as has already been requested by the Royals at Wimbledon.

We are obliged to convey to certain arrogant British types that we Americans have our Royalty, too. We Present, Lady Gaga! Does Her Majesty Queen Elizabeth wear a raw meat dress? Answer: No! A meat dress is useful for those occasions in life when one is attacked by cannibals. The Cannibal Gentlemen rip the meat dress off, and gnaw on the dress, while Her Majesty runs off, her dignity intact.

Australia's Northern Territory should be an Australian, UACBAS state. Why? Two U.S. senators. Power. World power.

Every embassy and consulate would remain, for at least 25 years. No closings at all. No job losses. Because: the UACBAS nation would be so huge and powerful. Every foreign office would remain. Same reason. For example, Whitehall could be responsible for UACBAS Europe relations. Australia, New Zealand for UACBAS Western and Southern Pacific. When you sort of shoulder the world, offices are necessary.

Every intelligence agency remains. No changes except huge growth in power, by interconnectedness with each other, with the CIA and the NSA and DIA and so on. MI6 is great, 007 is there, handling things. Bond, James Bond, Tomorrow Never Dies. Thank-you, James. Well done.

The UACBAS proposal can begin with a billion dollar trust. The trust can sponsor a continuing, unending series of meetings of various groups from the United States, Canada, Britain, Ireland, Australia, New Zealand, Liberia, Puerto Rico, Singapore. Including members of Congress and of the Parliaments. All featured on the evening news, month after month.

The groups can be seen visiting the major cities and sites of each nation, *with their families*. The Grand Canyon. Ayers Rock. The Sydney Opera House. Houses of Parliament, Westminster Abbey, and other historic sites in London. The Emerald Isle. Las Vegas. Disney World. Beautiful sites of New Zealand. Glorious Canada. Beautiful Ottawa. Vancouver harbor. San Juan. Miami. The great national parks. And so on.

U.S. Black leaders visit Liberia. Very profound.

Groups from these nations, travelling to the other nations, can be such as, Business leaders. Doctors. Leading women. University Student Presidents. Members of Congress and of the Parliaments. University presidents. Local television reporters. Editors. Columnists. Protestant and Catholic and Jewish clergy separately and together. Black leaders. Hispanic leaders. Celebs. All of this, top of the evening news in each of the UACBAS nations.

Suuuper!Party! supports testing the proposal.

Each of Britain, Ireland, Canada, Australia, New Zealand, et al, that now do not have a National Football League team, a Major League Baseball team, a National Hockey League team, and a National Basketball Association team, would get one. Each team would be *publicly-owned*, like the Green Bay Packers. Cricket, naah. And a MAiNGlobal Football/Soccer Team, as a national team, Chapter Fifteen.

All this nation-building is hugely important. It is important to the nations involved. It is important to the world. It is emotionally moving. It is the creation of: **The Greatest Nation in History**. By far. It is an advantage to all peaceful nations. The UACBAS nation could grow to one billion in population. Lots of room to grow.

The Immense Nation is Small Compared to 1776

In 1776, to travel from some places in America to another took two weeks, a brutal two weeks on spine-jarring, teeth-rattling tracks, a jar inside the stagecoach for Number 1, behind the trees in the snow for Number 2.

Today, Boston is much, much closer to Sydney and London and Liberia, *only hours away*, than it was to Atlanta in 1776, *days away*.

Each nation in the federation enormously increases its population and geographic area. And power and variety.

Each nation *is* Millions of Square Miles.

Congratulations to the citizens of each nation on becoming the World Superpower, indeed the unchallengeable Global Hyperpower, a benign influence for the world.

The leading political party in the UACBAS could well be the hybrid Suuuper!Party!, that is, hybrid with each of the other parties. Suuuper!Party!-Liberal candidates and Suuuper!Party!-Conservative candidates in Britain, and so on in each nation.

Suuuper!Party! offers the unique, historic, liberating, and inviting Real Egalitarianism, and Free University Education for All Forever. And the World Parliament of Women. And UACBAS. Unmatchable all. No other party can compete.

President of the United States

The UACBAS would mean, on regular occasion a British man or woman as President of the United States. As long as he does not say loo. UACBAS means, on occasion a Canadian man or woman as President of the United States, eh? UACBAS means, on occasion an Australian man or woman as President of the United States, probably Russell Crowe. We suppose that Prince Harry would be a candidate who could beat any other, providing that he is married, to a strong woman. UACBAS means, on occasion a Kiwi man or woman as President of the United States. UACBAS means, on occasion a Singaporean man or woman as President of the United States. Better not cross President Lee, or judicial caning!

Problems Problems

The UACBAS nation would require its own, um, CONGRESS & PARLIAMENTS AIR, with a fleet of Gulfstream 650s, flying constantly, 24/7, on a circuit to and from America, Canada, Britain, Ireland, Australia, New Zealand, Liberia, Puerto Rico, Singapore. To the capital cities and to the largest cities.

What a burden of Office. Congress & Parliaments Air, for members of Congress and of the Parliaments. Somehow, the members of Congress and of the Parliaments would need to take on this stern duty, indeed shoulder this heavy weight of High Office, having their own airline. Duty, Honor! For God and Country! Rule Brittania! O Canada! Advance Australia Fair! God Defend New Zealand! England expects that every man will do his duty!

No, Sir, you certainly may not grab an Air Congress, 'Gee6' as you put it, to go visit Barbie Big Ones on Bondi Beach in Sydney. That is an outrage against proper use. Thank-you very much! Instead, say that you are going to examine a coal mine in Perth.

Another burden of high office is shouldering the responsibilities of the 100,000,000 MAiN Perpetual Seat Trust for each Congressional and Parliamentary seat, and its millions a year in income for each member, for Good Works and Personal Expenditures.

Is there simply no limit to the Herculean Tasks, indeed sufferings, indeed Noble Labors for Our Benefit, that must be taken up by those in High Office? Soldier on, O Great Statespersons!

History Calls, Whatever That Means

What is the chance of creating this far and away greatest nation in history, a 75-state United America Canada Britain AustraliaNZ States? No mortal knows.

There is the historical precedent of a grateful nation giving Blenheim Palace to the Duke of Marlborough, an award for having won the great-for-its-time, now obscure, Battle of Blenheim, in 1704. Google, Blenheim Palace photos. It might be possible to give mere, high eight-figure National Honor Awards, a Perpetual Family Trust, to each Member of Parliament and of Congress upon the Greatest Federation in History being achieved, before an awestruck world, and a grateful nation.

These would be Historic Honor Awards for: Creating the Greatest Nation in History by far, for the Statesmen and Stateswomen creating The Only Nation On Which The Sun Never Sets.

The Only Nation that Amazes the World.

This would be as inexpensive as paying only $7,000,000 to purchase Alaska in the Alaska Purchase of 1867, or the Louisiana Purchase in 1803 for a mere $15,000,000, for an area that covers all or part of 15 present U.S. states and two Canadian provinces.

When the U.S. paid $15,000,000 to create much of the nation in 1803, the entire annual federal budget was $8.2 million (not a typo). That is, the U.S. paid only twice its annual budget to buy 15 states. This is equivalent in today's terms to spending $6 Trillion dollars ($6,000,000,000,000, not a typo).

Therefore, to give National Honor Awards to each of say, 5,000 federal legislators in the nations, to award Perpetual Family Trusts of even $100,000,000 to each member of Parliament and Congress, and to Cabinet Officers, $500,000,000,000 ($500 billion total, a lousy $50 bill a year for ten years) would be *really cheap*, compared to the annual national budget of over $3 Trillion in the U.S. alone. Moreover, the modest, little, small, insignificant $500 Billion dollars would be spent and saved and invested in the UACBAS, a help to the economy. Tax-free. It is a one-time only expense with truly epic, huge history results, and popular benefit.

Five hundred Billion dollars in National Honor Awards for: Changing all History. For *Reshaping the World*. For Benefitting Humanity. It is dirt cheap, a minor bookkeeping matter. National Honor Awards for Great Achievements of the Ages are normal. People get used to a changed landscape.

Human beings, including federal legislators, are variously persnickety, provincial, stubborn, pompous, pretentious, precious, secretly angry, openly angry, blind, hidden hostile, obstinate, malicious, foot-dragging, lazy, resentful, swaggering lout men, girling-out women, cowardly cautious, all the usual clutter of human nature. National Honor Awards cut through all these 1,000 clutter items to make an immense historical achievement. Corporations pay officers and employees to overcome the same above-noted marvelous human natures.

The major players in the UACBAS would be **Founding Fathers II and The Historic Founding Women**.

Prominent Women: It is important that prominent women step up. Suggestion, get your swagger on. Swagger it out. That is what the Dominant, Winner, Power men are going to do. So they can achieve and, um, dominate. In due course, the Men of Power square their shoulders, and say among themselves, "Oh eff it, let's just do it. Charge forward."
Will you be there, Triumphant with History's Winners?
Or will you be doing loser deep-girlism?
Abigail Adams wrote to John Adams in 1776, "...in the new code of laws...I desire you would remember the ladies..." John did not. All the more reason for prominent women to be Strong Women. Step up toughly. Frown. Gravitas, not grinning. Set your jaw. Do it for women. Put yourself forward. Say to some men, "To hell with weaklings. Right?" Scare 'em.
It is also important that Black leaders and others step up to be the supra-historic, Founding Fathers II and The Founding

Women. Suggestion, swagger it out. Making history is fun. You get all the loot.

It is unfortunate that Russia is not English-speaking. As seen on a world map.

A Republican or Democratic hybrid-Suuuper!Party! President of the United States could and, uh, would convene monthly meetings of the Prime Ministers, and of the Cabinets, and major Parliament members, and attend such meetings convened by Prime Ministers, in London, Canberra and the other capitals. The world watches. Fascinated. Spellbound. Captivated. Depressed. Envious.

Founding Fathers II and The Historic Founding Women

The Parliamentary and Congressional vote to create the nation would be SIMULTANEOUS in each nation, counting One-Member-By-One-Member-At-A-Time, in one nation after the other. Then, the second member serially voting in each nation, then the third member voting in each nation, and so on.

THE ENTIRE WORLD WOULD WATCH, UTTERLY TRANSFIXED, EVERY CABINET AND PARLIAMENT ON THE PLANET HOLDING ITS BREATH, each human being on earth knowing that History Is Being Made, that the world is being changed forever, for the better.

YOU? You creating, **The Greatest Nation Ever.**

YOU? creating, **The Only Nation On Which The Sun Never Sets**.

Consider the magnitude of the achievement.

The U.S. would be the world hyperpower. The United America Canada Britain AustraliaNZ States nation, UACBAS, would be the anchor nation of the world.

The UACBAS *transforms the world*. And transforms the lives of its citizens.

As Hegel said, "America is therefore the land of the future, where, in the ages that lie before us, the burden of the World's History shall reveal itself." Let pouters pout.

Walter Lohman, director of the Asian Studies Center at the Heritage Foundation, April 8, 2013, "American leadership has brought about the most peaceful, prosperous, and free world in the history of mankind." LPP.

POSTSCRIPT: **The Most Powerful and Richest Billion People On Earth:** The case can be made that The Mutual Advantage Population of the UACBAS could number One Billion People on Day One: the UACBAS plus the Americas: Latin America from the Rio Grande to Argentina and Chile, the Caribbean nations, and Iceland and Greenland.

There are some civilizational and good fortune common denominators among these nations. Fabulous good fortune: each nation is surrounded by one or two oceans.

Therefore, there can be a monthly **Common Civilization Assembly** by these nations, Presidents and Prime Ministers, sometimes all-cabinets meetings, sometimes in D.C. and Rio and Mexico City and Ottawa and Buenos Aires and Santiago and....sometimes in London and Canberra and Wellington, and Reykjavik and Godthab in summertime. This means the world amazed, and even reshaped. A de facto **Super SuperPower.** Copying the European Union meetings even when no English-speaking nation is present, um, after ten years, English-speakers only. History will absolve us!

The President of China would be invited to sit-in as an observer of our plots. Especially if he brings Sichuan.

On the agenda of the Common Civilization Assembly:

(1) The Revolution Against Caste, the Historic Civil Rights Act for Real Egalitarianism with the Sixteen Basic Guarantees for Parents. (2) Free Streaming University for All Human Beings Forever. Including one world-university in Spanish, from Mexico City, and one in Portuguese from Rio de Janeiro. (3) Democracy for non-democratic regimes. (4) Free trade. (5) Defense. Joint air-land-sea-space exercises.

(6) Selection of a Universal Second Language to be taught in all Common Civilization schools, providing it is the USL chosen by Chile, South Korea, Singapore, Hong Kong, the Philippines, India, northern Europe, the world's elite, 300,000,000 Chinese, and begins with the letter 'E'.

The above-noted offers a treasure trove of material for YouTube and Facebook and Twitter entrants in the opportunity to apply for very large awards that might be paid out. Fun Disruptor Awards Chapter Thirty.

Fun Disruptor
Chapter Twenty-five

The Twentieth of Twenty-three Currency-Validations by World Treasury Bank MAiN that Really Please Humanity.

This is How Billionaires Can Be Acclaimed Worldwide for Decades by Popular, Liberating Actions from World Treasury Bank, the MAiN, and its Founders.

HOW TO END ALMOST ALL GUN VIOLENCE IN AMERICA

Ninety-nine percent (99%) of gun violence in America is committed by No-School-Homeworked men murdering No-School-Homeworked men. These are facts-on-the-ground. This is not a theory. It is purely factual.

Juan Williams has noted in the Wall Street Journal, that 44,038 black children have been killed by guns since 1979. This is a "slaughter", as Mr. Williams notes. What Juan Williams, who is a man of wisdom, nevertheless did not notice is that 99% if not in fact 99.9% of these murders come from No-School-Homeworked males murdering No-School-Homeworked males.

Thanks, teachers unions.

It is not that School Homeworked males are more virtuous than No School Homeworked makes. Most all males essentially want to kill the guy who flips them off, cuts them off, calls them a lower bodily orifice, looks at them the wrong way, and so on. It is that the mandatory school homeworked males are on a different life trajectory. They shrug off rather than escalate. It is, 'I have a future' versus 'I have no future'.

Juan Williams has said that the murder rate by and of black males is high. Actually, this is not true at all, Mr. Williams. **The murder rate by Mandatory School Homeworked Black males is essentially zero**, sort of like the murder rate by Mandatory School Homeworked Jewish males, which is almost a stand-up comedian's joke, and by Mandatory School Homeworked Asian-American males.

Mandatory School Homeworked black males are not being killed by anyone, nor are they killing anyone. They are in college, going to the Big Game with a cute coed, hoping to get lucky.

There are no Mandatory School Homeworked gangs. Not one.

Mandatory school homeworked gangs are known as... University Fraternities.

Therefore, to end almost all gun violence in America, what is needed is the Real Egalitarianism of access by 100% of parents to Mandatory School Homework Schools, at Top World Class Level, beginning at grade one, in which the parent-chosen school takes 100% of the responsibility to supervise that the school homework is done 200 times a year, for 12 years, 2,400 times.

In Education, Black Leaders Should Declare Independence and Autonomy

Black leaders and teachers should break with teachers unions that are lost in the candy-floss, addle-brained, goofy-land of "inspiring the children to learn." The culture that invented the phrase, 'a good whuppin', is not scared of offering Mandatory School Homework Schools to parents.

Black America is currently the victim of a terrible whuppin' from the pitilessly stupid regime of the fantasies of pablum-sociology. These fantasies are, Inspiring the children to learn. The feeble, sad, 'Sparking an interest'. (Boys have their interest in science sparked. One boy bends over and rips out a big one. The other boys try to light it on fire. Well, at least it's a chemistry experiment. Look on the positive side).

No Child Left Behind means 50,000,000 children left behind.

There is the hapless, silly and meaningless, Race to the Top. Compelling attentiveness during classes, and imposing Mandatory School Homework, is not a goofy 'race to the top'.

Teaching is patient slogging by serious, suspicious adults. All the Age of Aquarius, intellectual gloppola is an embarrassment to the U.S., and a catastrophe for lower-middle-class and poor families.

As noted, *the Major Producers of Poverty in America are: the Teachers Unions*. Semi-literacy causes poverty.

Consider: All Humanity is divided between the people Up There and the people Down There. The sole, decisive dividing line is not anything but: Mandatory School Homework Schooling by the People Up There. They are not brilliant.

Black leaders, and Hispanic groups, should grimly insist that Congress pass, **The Historic Civil Rights Act for Real Egalitarianism**, Year 20___, with, **The Sixteen Basic Guarantees to Parents**. Fun Disruptor Chapters Seventeen and Eighteen.

Coldly, absolutely, insist on 1. Auditing of School Homework *individually*, and daily (not monthly, nor seasonally) and, 2. Parental Right to Benchmarking, to compare the daily homework assignments in Singapore, 200 times a year for 12 years. And that their child can daily see DVDs of the Singaporean classes behind the homework.

Suggestion for meetings with educrats, <u>refuse to smile</u>. Refuse to chuckle. *The dominant culture always wants the disempowered to laugh easily and chuckle at their sad, disempowered situation.*

The Sixteen Basic Guarantees to Parents, seen in Fun Disruptor Chapter Seventeen, cause fear and trembling, and deep anger, in the pantywaist set. However, without each and all of these Parental Rights, it will be a continuation of the Classist, Caste System Regime, which is, Mathematics and the Sciences for white, blonde, upper-middle-class and wealthy students, the children of ambitious professionals. For the children of color: Simple arithmetic and green glop, save-the-planet religion.

(If any of the Sixteen is sacrificed, the other fifteen collapse, like a three-legged stool with only two legs).

The current dominant culture is willing to sucker-in Black and Hispanic Americans and working class whites to be an *Under-educated Underclass, Dependent* on the government, and thus captive voters for politicians who believe that These Voters Are Stupid, *Not In-tell-i-gent Enough*. Here is what the Classist, No-school-homework for people of color and for all lower-middle class and middle-middle class Americans does: makes them quarter-educated helpless. So, smile not. Be not friendly. Loudly complain about frivolous demeanor. **Ask**

loudly, especially on television, 'You find this national crisis and disaster for us to be *amusing*??'

Arrange visits to Singapore educators. We invite Singaporean educators to come up with <u>The Complete List of School Homework Assignments</u>, in all subjects, 200 times a year, for 12 years, along with the expected hours of school homework for each assignment. And DVDs of each and every class being taught over twelve years.

In all probability the U.S. teachers unions will respond by dancing with joy and bursting into song, or, suicidal thoughts and going real heavy on the Johnny Black.

Let grim, justifiably angry Black and Hispanic leaders and many others insist on Equality in American schools with the World-Top-Class Benchmarking Standards, five times a week, 200 times a year, 2,400 times over 12 years of grade school.

The current indifference to teaching Inner City Black Americans how to read and compose essays and do mathematics must be stopped, and there must be substantial Apology-Remorse Payments to Black leaders and civil rights organizations. The insults are too great. The damage is too great.

Enough, enough and way too much Caste System cruelty.

If you are a Black or Hispanic leader, and you are not grimly angry about the destruction of a prosperous future for Black America every school night, the destruction of a prosperous future for Hispanic America every school night, the destruction of a prosperous future for Blue collar and Pink collar America every school night, and the destruction of a prosperous future for much of White suburban America every school night, what is wrong with you? Just anger is just.

Twelve cheerful words that every Black leader can enjoy saying every day: "The crime rate by Mandatory School Homeworked Black males is essentially zero."

Mandatory School Homework provides, Living Large. Mandatory School Homework provides, The Best Revenge.

The Historic Civil Rights Act for Real Egalitarianism, Year 20___, and, The Sixteen Basic Guarantees to Parents, hugely empower teachers who can bring themselves to abandon the *cruelly mindless*, Marshmallow One, "inspiring the children to learn" and the deep doo-doo of Marshmallow Two, "sparking an interest."

Oh puhleeze! The boys respond by smirking and will not have it.

Teachers, at long last, have you no sense of shame?

At long, long last, grow up, at long last, GROW UP.

The above-noted offers a treasure trove of material for YouTube and Facebook and Twitter entrants in the opportunity to apply for very large awards that might be paid out. Fun Disruptor Awards Chapter Thirty.

Fun Disruptor
Chapter Twenty-six

The Twenty-first of Twenty-three Currency-Validations by World Treasury Bank MAiN that Really Please Humanity.

This is How Billionaires Can Be Acclaimed Worldwide for Decades by Popular, Liberating Actions from World Treasury Bank, the MAiN, and its Founders.

HOW GREATLY TO REDUCE OBESITY IN AMERICA

Obesity is not distributed equally among all social groups in America. This can be noticed. Many observers might agree with the following: If one were to line up 1,000 randomly chosen university graduates, obesity, defined as not merely being a few pounds overweight, but obesity as described by most anyone as "he's fat" or "he's really fat", would be relatively rare.

University graduates have a cultural common denominator: Mandatory School Homework 200 times a year for twelve years in school.

In contrast, one could rudely point out, if we look at 1,000 randomly selected No-School-Homeworked adults, often high school dropouts, the rate of obesity and gross obesity skyrockets.

If these observations are true, two obvious questions arise: What possible connection can there be between Mandatory School Homeworked adults and obesity being uncommon among them? And, what possible connection can there be between No School Homeworked adults and obesity and gross obesity being common among them?

We Do Not Know. So here are our guesses. The Mandatory School Homeworked adults are simply on a different life trajectory. Maybe they go into businesses and professions and lifestyles where a reasonably trim figure is expected or customary. Maybe they read the health articles in newspapers. Maybe they pay more attention to the health tips on television news.

Whatever the case, the Real Egalitarianism of access by 100% of parents to Mandatory School Homework Schools, as provided by Suuuper!Party!, would stand to reduce the obesity problem substantially. Fun Disruptor Chapters Seventeen and Eighteen.

Trying to get people who never watch even television news to eat healthy? Fat chance of that. Pass the potato chips.

It is unfortunate in our view that the anti-obesity crusade by First Lady Michelle Obama, whom we admire, does not include the far more important arranging of the Real Egalitarianism of access by 100% of parents to Mandatory School Homework Schools, at Top World Class Level. For, to achieve the obvious goal of parents having such access, beginning at grade one, seems to promise a large reduction in the obesity epidemic.

How Michelle Obama Can Make Some History

It would be a great help to many tens of millions of families, and a great increase in family prosperity, if the First Lady decided to end the awful, pathetic nonsense that success in grade school education is about "inspiring the children to learn". We have noted elsewhere that this foolishness, just for starters, excludes boys, and greatly wounds their families.

Our respectful suggestion is to arrange passage of **The Historic Civil Rights Act for Real Egalitarianism, Year 20___**. Including, **The Sixteen Basic Guarantees to Parents**. Fun Disruptor Chapters Seventeen and Eighteen.

This would make First Lady Obama one of the great, world leaders of our era.

The above-noted offers a treasure trove of material for YouTube and Facebook and Twitter entrants in the opportunity to apply for very large awards that might be paid out. Fun Disruptor Awards Chapter Thirty.

Fun Disruptor
Chapter Twenty-seven

The Twenty-second of Twenty-three Currency-Validations by World Treasury Bank MAiN that Really Please Humanity.

This is How Billionaires Can Be Acclaimed Worldwide for Decades by Popular, Liberating Actions from World Treasury Bank, the MAiN, and its Founders.

We just kind of throw this section into the mix. Some people might regard it as sort of blather. Then again, maybe something may come of this proposal. The bored reader can skip this chapter.

To further empower World Treasury Bank and the MAiN, and to constitute a MAiN Currency-Validation unto itself, there can be in Beijing or wherever:

THE ANNUAL CONVENING OF WORLD LEADERS

The Money Summit, in Beijing or wherever it occurs, is to result in World Treasury Bank issuing perhaps 100 Trillion MAiN over a period of some years of the world's first, true World Currency. The World Treasury Bank MAiN Summit may be held annually.

To add Gravitas and Solemnity, and *Power that Cannot Be Outflanked* by potential business competitors, in the Second Money Summit, "The World's Leaders" can be convened, by World Treasury Bank MAiN, and by Suuuper!Party!, along with both other U.S. parties, and the U.S. administration, and Major Media, with Worldwide Commentary TV Newscasts, on a continuing basis.

Invited from 150+ Nations Can Be:

ONE:

All **Federal Legislators**, from Congress and the Parliaments, of 150+ nations. <u>And their families</u>, their spouses and kids. For examples: all members of Congress, all members of the European Union parliaments, all parliament members of India, all members of China's National People's Congress, and the National Committee of the Chinese People's Political Consultative Conference. Say, 500 Parliament and Congress members from 150 nations equals 75,000 national legislators. The World Economic Forum, Davos and Dalian, may be looked upon as inspiration for The World Treasury Bank MAiN Annual Convening of the World's Leaders.

Cabinet officers can make big-screen presentations.

This alone, gathering together all national legislators, is a first in history, and, if achieved, would actually be *One of the Most Momentous Events In History*. Perhaps *The* Most Momentous Event In History.

Wouldn't it? Has there ever been anything larger by mortals? If so, what?

TWO:

All retired heads of government and state, that is, former Presidents and Prime Ministers.

THREE:

Fully 100,000 Editors, Columnists, TV News Anchors, Reporters. 10,000 Radio Talk Show hosts broadcasting live from, say, Tiananmen Square. Those invited can receive $1,000,000 MAiN Issuance Awards each. They will be there.

FOUR:

The World's 1,426 Billionaires. The CEOs and Board Members of the world's largest 2,000 corporations, and 1,000 largest banks. The presidents and board members of 1,000 labor unions.

The Boards of the 100 Largest Media Corporations on earth. Each Board is to receive a One Billion MAiN World Honor Award for the Board. Chapter Five. The Honor Award is for supporting World Treasury Bank MAiN University, which is, **Free University, For All Human Beings, Forever**. And for supporting, **The End of the 5,000-year Caste System in Education**, the liberation of humanity by the Revolution Against Caste, known as the Real Egalitarianism of access by 100% of parents to Mandatory School Homework Schools, at Top World Class Level, in which the school takes 100% of the responsibility to supervise that the school homework is done.

FIVE:

Leaders of 1,000 <u>non-nation</u> social groups. For example, Indians of Peru. And so on.

SIX:

The **World Parliament of All Women**, with its five hundred Members of Parliament elected online. The Chancellor of the World Parliament of Women and the Women's Parliament Chancellors of each continent and of India and China. The World Parliament of Women will, unsuspected, be able to wield actually-immense power, by a worldwide boycott of all the products of a selected nation that oppresses women.

SEVEN:
10,000 University Presidents. 10,000 Police Chiefs. 10,000 Judges. 10,000 Military Officers.

Thousands of celebrities. Movie stars. Music stars. Sports stars.

A Celebratory Occasion

The Annual Convening of World Leaders in Beijing or wherever, can have a *celebratory* atmosphere. For example, Hundreds of scanning Searchlights piercing the sky from Tiananmen Square. Food fairs. Singers singing in dozens of concerts. Nation-concerts: America. Brazil. Israel. Argentina. South Africa. Britain, and others.

And a huge Art Fair, art for display and for sale, artists from 150+ nations, in alphabetical order by nation. And so on.

The idea is that, risking blather here, try to forgive, the Convening of the World Leaders is to be held Annually, "for 1,000 Years", long after the issuance of the First True World Currency, the MAiN. The years are to be numbered, for example: "Year One of 1,000 Years." And so on.

All of the above may prove to be as beneficial for humanity as the great revolutions of 1776 and 1789.

Founders of World Treasury Bank can be as proud to be associated with these historic advances for humanity as your great, great grandchildren will be of you.

The above-noted offers a treasure trove of material for You-Tube and Facebook and Twitter entrants in the opportunity to apply for very large awards that might be paid out. Fun Disruptor Awards Chapter Thirty.

A BORING, BLATHER ITEM:
AFTER CENTURIES, A NEW, OPTIONAL CALENDAR

The Annual Convening Of World Leaders can review this idea.

This is meant to be: Merely a harmless idea, no more.

World Smartphones allow the creation of an OPTIONAL new world calendar of 13 months of 28 days each, equals 364 days. With one Leap Day per year.
(As some people suffer from Triskaidekaphobia, the thirteenth month can be referred to as Extra Month. Oh gosh.)

The new calendar can be just a simple, free, *tiny app*. Downloaded with the World Treasury Bank MAiN apps downloaded to 3,000,000,000 smartphone owners.

The Extra Month, named the universally-attractive Laurel, can come in the northern hemisphere summer, after August. .....June, July, August, Laurel, September...

Some people might be attracted to all months being 28 days, and to having an extra summer month each year. Others, not.

Each Smartphone user can:

Choose *always to ignore and never once look at* the New World Calendar. This is fine. Or,

Have both calendar dates on his or her Smartphone screen, or,

Toggle between the calendars at will.

Will such a New World Calendar become a world standard? Nobody knows.

It may be a dud. If so, no harm done.

Anyway, it may be a great legacy for one's great, great grandchildren. They can talk about your involvement in the New World Calendar.

The above-noted offers a treasure trove of material for You-Tube and Facebook and Twitter entrants in the opportunity to apply for very large awards that might be paid out. Fun Disruptor Awards Chapter Thirty.

Chapter Twenty-Eight
JEFFREY BEZOS SHOULD RECEIVE THE PRESIDENTIAL MEDAL OF FREEDOM

The Presidential Medal of Freedom is an award bestowed by the President of the United States and is, along with the comparable Congressional Gold Medal bestowed by an act of U.S. Congress, the highest civilian award in the United States. It recognizes those individuals who have made "an especially meritorious contribution to the security or national interests of the United States, world peace, cultural or other significant public or private endeavors." The preceding paragraph is from Wikipedia.

In our view, Amazon.com founder and chief executive Jeffrey Bezos deserves such a national honor.

Among the reasons, Jeffrey Bezos has revolutionized book publishing from the standpoint of authors. Throughout gloomy centuries, since the invention of the printing press, book authors have been hapless supplicants standing before the book publishers rather as Oliver Twist begging for more soup in the orphanage.

Upon finally getting one of the Lord High Publishers to publish the pitiful scribe's pathetic masterpiece, there then followed a Dickensian, plodding process that sometimes took such as two years to finally plop out the book.

Until Jeffrey Bezos. The Founder, Chairman and Chief Executive Officer of Amazon.com created the self-published book, at Amazon's CreateSpace.com, and its stunning Print On Demand aspect. These have enormously empowered both book authors and their readers. Books should be and we predict will be written about Mr. Bezos' historic achievement.

Mr. Bezos' other world-changing achievements include the building of Amazon.com. The book-selling part of Amazon.com ended the used-to-be six to eight week wait for a bookstore to obtain a book that the helpless, pathetic boob customer ordered.

Amazon.com also allowed customers all over the world to see hundreds or thousands of selections of a topic that interested the book buyer, rather than the hapless reader happening to see a book mentioned in the Sunday paper book review.

Jeffrey Bezos has also started a space company "to help enable anyone to go into space." All we ask is that Mr. Bezos not go there himself. We need his continued accomplishments here on earth.

This from Business Insider founder-editor, Henry Blodget: "Jeff Bezos's leadership, vision, and philosophy at Amazon over the last two decades have inspired a whole generation of start-ups and entrepreneurs, including me. Jeff has always put Amazon's customers first. This focus is rare in American business, and it is one reason why Amazon has been so successful. I have admired Jeff and Amazon since the mid-1990s, and it is a privilege and pleasure to have Jeff invest in the company. Obviously, at Business Insider, we write about Amazon occasionally, along with some of Jeff's other ventures (rockets, rocket engines, and other cool stuff.) In the future, our articles on these topics will disclose that Jeff is an investor in the company."

Jeffrey Bezos should receive the Presidential Medal of Freedom.

Fun Disruptor
Chapter Twenty-nine

The Twenty-third of Twenty-three Currency-Validations by World Treasury Bank MAiN that Really Please Humanity.

This is How Billionaires Can Be Acclaimed Worldwide for Decades by Popular, Liberating Actions from World Treasury Bank, the MAiN, and its Founders.

THE GREATEST SPORTS LEAGUE EVER

After a Temporary Absence of 2,500 Years, League 4-Horse Chariot Racing is Back!

The League may be able to be a billion dollars a day business, 365 days a year.

The Sports League that May Become as Big as Exxon Mobil

This addendum, about a new, first ever, worldwide sports league is, in some ways only, tangential to this book. However, it does comport with the theme of making large fortunes for private equity. And making billions of people happy. Moreover, the Beneficial Automatic Individual Retirement Account for wagerers, below, comes under the heading of helping any number of people in every nation. And betting is by Debit Card only. No credit cards.

It can be asked, How can any suggestion sensibly be made that the revival of 4-horse chariot racing may be able to be a 'billion dollars a day' wagering sport?

Here is a reason. World 4-Horse Chariot Racing League is the only sport in history in which 200 Nations and Social Groups can compete nightly, 365 days a year. That is, say, 15 races nightly with fifteen, World 4-Horse Chariot Racing League teams in each race. Thus, **there may be 225 nations and social groups, in wild, pell-mell, frantic, heroic, compelling competition 365 nights a year.**

To speculate, consider that 50,000,000 people worldwide bet an average of $50 a day. *This would be $2,500,000,000 a day*, $912,500,000 billion dollars a year. Call it a trillion dollars. Such might occur in China alone.

The World 4-Horse Chariot Racing League could perhaps be founded by World Treasury Bank MAiN. We say 'perhaps' because a strong case can be made, should be made, and will be made, that a bank has no business being connected to a wagering sport. Yet there is a reason that national legislatures may support World 4-Horse Chariot Racing League.

For National Legislatures

There is a feature of the League that legislatures may appreciate. Here it is. The wagerer must put down 10% more than his bet. Bet $10.00, put down $11.00. This 10 percent goes into his or her **Beneficial Automatic Individual Retirement Account**, which is typically not accessible until age 65. This plan has something of the nanny aspect to it. However, it does take into account human failings and folly.

Say that Mr. Less-than-perfect Husband bets $100 a day for 40 years. His Beneficial Automatic Individual Retirement Account thereby gets $10.00 a day, $3,650.00 a year. Multiplied by 40 years this is $146,000.00. At, say, 5% compound interest over 40 years, this is, "Honey, we're rich!"

Some wagerers may choose to save, that is, invest more than ten percent on each bet. That is, contribute to their retirement fund.

The Bank and League both could obtain an incalculable amount of free advertising, in 150 nations, daily, for years and decades, IF the decision is made to have the league name, World 4-Horse Chariot Racing League from World Treasury Bank MAiN.

This is for collegial decision by the Major Players. The decision may be no.

If 10,000,000 people in China bet $100 a day, that is one billion dollars a day, $365 billion a year.

If 100,000,000 television fans of World 4-Horse Chariot Racing League worldwide wager an average of $10.00 a day each, that is one billion dollars a day, 365 days a year, $365 billion annually.

The *annual* gaming total for all of Las Vegas is about $10 Billion.

Some observers may care to speculate Blue Sky numbers that equal a trillion dollars a year. Say that 200,000,000 people worldwide wager only an average of $13.70 a day each. This is $2,740,000,000 a day. Multiplied by 365 days makes One Trillion Dollars a year. People can bet on their smartphones during lunch with friends.

Exxon Mobil's revenue in 2012 was U.S. $452 Billion, with net income of U.S. $41 Billion.

Say that 20,000,000 people worldwide wager an average of the above-noted $13.70 a day. This is $274,000,000 a day. Multiplied by 365 days makes One Hundred Billion dollars a year. Not a bad little business.

Of course, these numbers are purely speculative. Yet, there has never been a world sport where 150 to 200 nations, plus social groups, in advertiser-sponsored teams, can compete every night, 365 nights a year, in wheel-to-wheel, Mano-a-Mano duels where fans shout and scream with passion even in their own living rooms. "Honey, you are frightening the children. And please try to watch the language in front of the children." Dad tends to get overexcited when watching World 4-Horse Chariot Racing League racing. Wagering may be large.

Okay, a potential trillion dollar annual gross for World 4-Horse Chariot Racing League is reasonably called, "Aw, come on!" Yet, the world economy is now near $80 trillion a year and rising to $100 trillion a year. In our age of worldwide television, worldwide businesses, the Internet, and mobile banking, betting could be from billions of smartphones on a 365-day, worldwide sport with 200 nations and social groups competing nightly in breathlessly exciting, shout-your-lungs-out competition. It might be that World 4-Horse Chariot Racing League can, uniquely, become a trillion dollar a year sport and entertainment business.

In contrast, a huge and great corporation such as Exxon Mobil is nevertheless not everywhere in the world. Not in every home. Not on billions of smartphones. Not used every day by hundreds of millions of people. People buy gas only every so often, not daily, and may buy from competitors. World 4-Horse Chariot Racing League may have hundreds of millions of daily viewers, and no competitors in its own 4-Horse Chariot Racing League economic sector.

It is at least conceivable that World 4-Horse Chariot Racing League will become a trillion dollar a year enterprise. Okay, "Aw, come on!"

The World 4-Horse Chariot Racing League is actually named Celebrities World 4-Horse Chariot Racing League. This is just a name. Celebrities cannot be charioteers, except in celebrity-charioteer races, with celebs-laughing and having fun, and mugging for the television cameras. As seen herein, the *male charioteers need to be brutes*, 6-feet-4 or bigger, for the wild, whipping duels, of each other. Whipping each other, not the horses.

Every team is in the Women's 4-Horse Chariot Racing League, by being seeded regularly in the Women's League Tenth Race each night. No whipping of each other by women charioteers.

The World 4-Horse Chariot Racing League requires a *new-built* race track, to be built in Las Vegas, according to current plan. Here is the reason: no horse race track in the U.S. or in the world has a wide enough track, the surface where the horses race, to accommodate say 15 World 4-Horse Chariot Racing League chariots. The four horses race side-by-side, not two-in-front-of-two. This requires a track that is 60 horses wide.

Some horse race tracks in Asia have crowds of 250,000. The new-built raceway, to use the League's term for a race track, means to accommodate such crowds, perhaps visitors from all over the world, to see their Hero Charioteers ride to inevitable victory.

Each of the dozens of bars and restaurants in this gigantic raceway must have continually panning, streaming cameras, so people in any nation, planning a trip, can check out family-friendly establishments at the raceway from those inhabited by baying males, yelling and shouting, sometimes using foul language, and being watched by 300-pound bouncers. Each restaurant and bar must post its full menu, with prices guaranteed to a specified date, on their raceway site.

The new-built raceway may be financed by an Initial Public Offering. Or perhaps better, by a real estate investment trust, perhaps selling grandstand seats, for their income. Say, 100,000 seats, sold for their daily income for a period of years, sold at, just say for example, $25,000 each. 100,000 times $25,000 equals in this purely speculative example, $2,500,000,000. The name of the raceway is, **O BEHOLD! O The World's Great Raceway!**

The League Can Be 100% Self-financing

Yet, **O Behold Raceway** might best be built from the plan to charge each of 1,000 Team Development Groups $25,000 more than the previous buyer paid, for a Team Development Group Racing Medallion. There are to be 1,000 Team Racing Medallions.

That is, the First Buyer of a Team Racing Medallion pays $25,000, the next pays $50,000 and so on up to the 1,000th Buyer pays $25,000,000. This totals $12,500,000,000 from the 1,000 buyers. A truly world stunning, 10-figure, O Behold Raceway can be built with some of such billions.

A Celebrities World 4-Horse Chariot Racing Team must own a Team Racing Medallion to race in any race ever.

The above plan means that the early purchasers may judge that the value of their Team Racing Medallion increases with each next purchase. In our view, the Team Advertiser Sponsor should pay the Team Racing Medallion fee retroactively.

What would cause an individual investor or corporation to invest, say, $25,000,000 for a Celebrities World 4-Horse Chariot Racing League Team Racing Medallion? Because each team is advertiser sponsored. According to Forbes, the average NASCAR team banks $12.3 million in annual profits. $25,000,000 might prove to be cheap. Or maybe not.

Are these Team Racing Medallions available at this time? Yes. WCRL# 0001 to WCRL# 1,000.

It might be that a Team Owner can make millions of dollars a year from its sponsor. A World 4-Horse Chariot Racing League Team makes the Greatest Advertising Vehicle Ever. A team can have One Sponsor Only, and can be designed and dedicated and uniformed and colored, front-to-back, for that sponsor.

One thousand teams may seem like a lot. Yet, Thoroughbred horse racing meets often have over 1,000 horses. There may be 15 races a day with 15 teams, 225 teams racing per day. Your team may race once every two weeks, or once a week. One thousand teams is only an average of ten teams from 100 nations. The U.S. alone may want to have 1,000 teams. There will need to be limited allocations per nation.

There stands to be a tremendous amount of excitement for the individuals who own a team that is seen weekly on worldwide television by persons in 200 nations and social groups. To speculate, there may develop a waiting list to buy Team Racing Medallions, and to form Team Development Groups.

The actual, physical medallion of each Team Racing Medallion can be privately commissioned by the Team Racing Medallion owner. It will have your Team Medallion Number, WCRL# 0001 to WCRL# 1,000 on it. It can be a medallion like a heavyweight boxing champion's belt. Or a large and strikingly ornate gold cup with 4-horse figurines on it. Two meters high, great. Go for it. Medallion-makers can advertise their fantastic productions on the League site. The very stylized horses of the Apollo Fountain at Versailles would look great on such a cup.

Las Vegas hotels around O Behold! can have moving sidewalks to O Behold!. Each hotel can own the property on which it is built.

O BEHOLD! O The World's Great Raceway! Now, that's a name. To be a 10-figure, world destination attraction, the architects will be given this marching order: MAKE FAMILIES GASP UPON SEEING O BEHOLD AND KIDS OPEN-MOUTHED WITH PLEASURE. The location may be in a valley. Tourists suddenly come upon it and are deeply pleased. And wowed. Air-conditioned grandstands, as in Qatar.

Inside, they will see their nation's heroic, 6-foot-6, 250-pound charioteer brute engaged in stunning, makes-even-grandma-shout her lungs out, wild, side-by-side, Mano a Mano, whipping duels, whipping each other with 15-foot long, thick, huge whips of various colors that could "strip the paint off a pick-up truck."

Crazy Wild Announcers

In most sports leagues, announcers and athletes both are not allowed to say that the other teams or the judges are cheating. In Celebrities World 4-Horse Chariot Racing League, announcers from 150+ nations, broadcasting from O Behold Raceway, broadcasting to back home, can screamingly accuse other teams and charioteers of cheating and unfairness and bias, and the charioteers can accuse other charioteers of cheating, unfair play, cowardice, and so on. There will be some 200 sports broadcast booths for sports reporters from every nation.

The announcers may be encouraged to *go bug-eyed with incredulity, and be open-mouthed, and smack their foreheads at witnessed perfidy.* (Just don't talk about the guy's mother or sisters. That crosses the line, even though, well, have you ever seen his sister? Hardcore!....). The fans will know that Celebrities World 4-Horse Chariot Racing League allows these cheerfully outrageous untruths to be said. Sample revelation, "It is tragic that this referee is obviously a blindfolded chimpanzee! Tragic!"

National patriotic gore can be very big, though supervised and kept in check by Celebrities World 4-Horse Chariot Racing League. Not a sipping mint juleps sport though.

If a team sponsor chooses, supporting announcers may interject at top lung, such as, "....showing colossal disrespect to what I happen to know for a fact is one of the finest products on earth... Furthermore, my dear, sainted mother uses this fabulous product! And I love my wonderful mother, as you love your wonderful mother! My outrage is great, as must be yours. Name-of-Product will not take this disrespect lying down!...... Their charioteer, Mr. Huge, must even the score, must!.... Or be seen as a coward......"

Fans will love all this cheerful throwing of trash-talk insults. The sponsors who choose the above option, if any, may really enjoy announcers and fans wearing sponsor colors and waving sponsor flags, shouting their "outraged" support of their sponsor and their great team and heroic, Mano a Mano battling charioteer. "We love you, Great Brutal!" "Please marry me, Mr. SuperBrute!, I love you!"

The Huge Guards had to have a talk with Her Ladyship about throwing her panties into Mr. SuperBrute!'s chariot. Mr. SuperBrute!'s ever-delicate sensibilities were unsettled, or at least Mrs. SuperBrute's delicate sensibilities were certainly unsettled. She did say something about, "I want to strangle that word-that-rhymes-with-bitch." Now, is that nice? Hey, it's

Celebrities World 4-Horse Chariot Racing League. Rock on! WE ARE THE CHAMPIONS!

Teams are encouraged to have cheerleaders. And also, rev-up-their-fans cheer leaders with bull-horns.

O BEHOLD! O The World's Great Raceway! will have a special seating section or suite for visiting heads of state and government, praying real hard for their Charioteer Heroes to win. The folks back home are watching. The Prime Minister does not want election defeat due to an under-performing, National Team heroic charioteer.

Gladiator Battles

Between races, there may be gladiator-like faux sword battles and the like between the typically 6-feet-4, 240-pound gladiators-charioteers. The teams and gladiator-charioteers represent: Nations, Sponsors, Ethnic groups. The gladiator-charioteers may 'fight' with light swords, as most races occur at night. It all stands to cause overwhelming emotions, revved up by crazy, wild announcers.

The O Behold! Great World Raceway may have "Devil's Holes", underground, horror caverns where reside ugly, slobbering, snotting beings who make The Alien creature look cuddly. They slither out nightly to wreak havoc.

The unfailing drama: a bunch of hero charioteers come together shoulder-to-shoulder due to the, "ALL Charioteers, Call to Action!! Call to Duty!! Call to Defend Civilization!!", repeated very loudly over and over on the public address system. They wield light-swords, as in Star Wars. The Hero Charioteers (Women, too) rush in, they come to the rescue, they force snarling, slobbering Devils back down into their Horror Caverns. However, children must not be frightened. Perhaps the slither people can be shown as smiling, genial guys putting on and taking off and putting on their head masks. "See, kids, we are really nice guys. We are just all having fun. Enjoy.".

Tourist trams can go down into the Horror Caverns on their tours of O Behold!.

Sometimes the Red Devil Racer Team runs races. He slobbers *a lot*. His mask is so ugly that he makes the Arkansas Razorback hog look like Gwyneth Paltrow in comparison. The Red Devil Racer Team is all crimson red: red-lighted chariot, red whip, red lighted uniform, red flying cape, red Seven League boots, red tack, the works. The fans loathe him with a rare passion. They call out, "Kill him! Kill him! Get him!" The Devil Racer not only cheats, he laughs fiendishly. Worse, his laugh is broadcast on the grandstand public address, and on worldwide television.

The Red Devil Racer, dressed all crimson red, likes to bend over and display his posterior to the fans, causing huge waves of enormous fun booing. After he wins a race, the charioteers gather together before a microphone, to apologize to the fans and say, "Don't worry. We'll get him next time!" Great fun. The Red Devil Racer's victories don't count in Triumph, Victory, Winner (win, place, show). He can't be bet on.

Good-bye to zebras with the pot-belly and big bum. The umpires, referees and judges can be in Darth Vader-ish costumes, seven-footers with light-swords. To show that Life Is Not Always Fair, when a Hero Charioteer is seen, and heard on the public address system, justifiably complaining to one of these gigantic, masked, impenetrable, ominous 'Referees', the referees may, obviously unfairly, incorrectly decide against the Hero Charioteer. And then may jump him and 'beat him'. Such scenarios need to be worked out so they please the fans, and can be explained to children.

The Old Judge. There can perhaps be such as an older, three hundred pound, white-wig wearing Supreme Court Judge, in his own Here Come de Judge chariot pulled by four little donkeys that the announcers invariably insist are "four magnificent steeds."

The judge wears inch-thick spectacles and carries an ever-ready quart of spirits. He reads the 2,500-page, 20-pound "The Book of Regulations" upside down before rendering dubious, sometimes unfair decisions, and then passing out.

On occasion, a television close-up shows a little mouse leaping out of the noble judge's barrister's wig.

On occasion, television close-ups show the judge receiving a one hundred dollar bill bribe slipped into his fat hand and him clumsily winking and nodding.

(The races themselves, being a wagering sport, must be literally F.B.I.-clean.).

If the reader has not seen 4-Horse Chariot Racing, or not seen recently, you can watch the famous nine-minute chariot racing scene in the winner of 11 Academy Awards motion picture, Ben-Hur. The DVD is available on Amazon.com.

The case can speculatively be made that Celebrities World 4-Horse Chariot Racing League might become worth a lot more than the National Football League, Major League Baseball, National Basketball Association and the National Hockey League, plus *all* the teams, all *combined*. Team owners in these sports should become equity owners in Celebrities World 4-Horse Chariot Racing League, obtaining a waiver as needed for being involved in a gambling sport.

The plan is to make this The Largest and Greatest Televised Sports League Ever.

Corporations and prominent individuals can then meet. A number of successive IPOs are planned in due course. The constituents of the League are three:

TEAMS:

The term team means: a Chariot and four Thoroughbred horses. Plus, numbers of spares for both. Each of these teams is has one-sponsor. *So owning and operating a team should costs the owner nothing.* At least that is the idea.

TRACKS, called RACEWAYS:

The raceway planned herein is **O BEHOLD! O The World's Great Raceway!** in or near Las Vegas.

Then perhaps other great destination raceways in future years.

TELEVISION:

Worldwide television from **O BEHOLD! Oh The World's Great Raceway!** for hours every day and night. Celebrities World 4-Horse Chariot Racing League racing can fill a worldwide television channel unto itself.

Costs in Celebrities World 4-Horse Chariot Racing League can be kept low by the simple means of low claiming prices on the horses. In contrast, it costs $15,000,000 to $25,000,000 a year to field a NASCAR team. The cars simply refuse to eat hay. They eat $100,000 engines like candy bars. Yet, as noted according to Forbes, the average NASCAR team banks $12.3 million in annual profits. Google, NASCAR team profits.

There is the possibility that TV ratings will make World 4-Horse Chariot Racing League the major sport in the world from its beginning.

The Senior League Executive

The current plan is to recruit a Fortune 500-genre, top performer, chief executive officer, perhaps give him potential 8 or 9-figures in stock options, to bring the Celebrities World 4-Horse Chariot Racing League into being, beginning with the design, worldwide review and critique of the design, then the building of the supra-magnificent, raises the bar, amazes the world, **O BEHOLD! O The World's Great Raceway!**

The League chief executive officer/commissioner can perhaps make early deals with one or more sports networks for worldwide telecasts with teams-from-150-nations from day one. League 4-horse chariot racing is *the sole available worldwide, universal-culture for 24 hours daily programming*, and the basis of international destination theme parks. Thus, chief executive officer of Celebrities World 4-Horse Chariot Racing League stands to be one of the *singular executive position open in the nation* today, and can perhaps make a fortune by any person's definition. The chief executive of a television network or other executive with national reputation can consider.

Potential Team Medallion owners can come forward. A list can be made of 1,000 potential team owners, and early bird purchasers.

The Next Great Franchise in the World Media Business

One:

Ownership of 2,000 hours and more a year of spectacular programming that every nation finds compellingly exciting. The basis for a branded television channel worldwide.

Two:

A MOTION PICTURE FRANCHISE: Modern 4-horse chariot racing makes a natural subject for a series of Rocky-genre motion pictures based on charioteer-gladiator heroes. There is a screenplay with sequel screenplays by an Oscar-nominated screenwriter.

Titles of the screenplays, Chariots of Thunder I. Chariots of Thunder II, Nine Lives to Live. Chariots of Thunder III, Death for Life.

These modern 4-horse chariot racing league screenplays are pure action, male macho, visceral combat stories for two, rival, two-fisted action heroes, with great girl friends.

Book Publishers: The Chariots of Thunder screenplays make a natural book franchise. Someone should write the novels. Action, glamor, love, fame, fortune, a global sport.

The Search For Motion Picture Franchises

It is rare to find a new motion picture subject that lends itself to sequels and is thus a franchise for a production company and a studio.

League 4-horse chariot racing is such a topic.

Moreover, Chariots of Thunder is a simple action, studio tentpole story.

Moreover, the story lends itself to the worldwide motion picture audience because the charioteer hero characters can be from each major motion picture nation.

How much can a genuinely new motion picture franchise add to the bottom line of a motion picture studio?

This is of course impossible to estimate, yet with, say, an original motion picture plus, with success, say two or three sequels or more of worldwide appeal, the amount might with good fortune equal a few high-grossing motion pictures. Worldwide.

Moreover, the nature of a World 4-Horse Chariot Racing League motion picture lends itself to motion picture *merchandise licensing*, toys, apparel, video games, restaurant chain promotions, and so on.

Possible TV Series

CARTOON SERIES: A <u>Chariots of Thunder</u> kids cartoon series.

TELEVISION SERIES: A <u>Chariots of Thunder</u> back-of-the-track television series.

STUDIO THEME PARK RIDES.

YOUNG CHARIOTEERS TV SERIES: A live-action TV series for the Power Rangers age group.

Three:

Entertainment corporations might come to own (1) Equity in a worldwide TV sports business and (2) A Destination-Attractions Business With Hotels with casinos, and (3) Equity in a Wagering Business, Second to None in Size, Celebrities World 4-Horse Chariot Racing League.

Four:

The League may become self-financed from 1,000 Team Development Groups' Racing Medallion fees. The result for an associated media corporation can be perhaps the largest entertainment, sports television and wagering business ever, and with a destination-attraction raceway, O Behold!.

Every major media corporation is attempting to obtain television programming that can be shown worldwide, to every continent and nation. Sports is the answer that they have decided upon. Yet, second-tier and third-tier sports are weak. Only the summer Olympics, which provides only 140 hours of television every four years, can be shown to a worldwide audience that appreciates the programming because nationals from their own nation are seen competing against others.

Now there can be a second such worldwide sport: Celebrities World 4-Horse Chariot Racing League racing. World 4-Horse Chariot Racing League racing can supply not 140 hours every four years but 2,000 hours and more every year of spectacularly exciting television for worldwide telecast.

O Behold! Raceway, may be open 24 hours a day, 365. It's Vegas.

The Idea in One Sentence, the Elevator Pitch

One of the signs of a business plan of the first rank is that it can be stated in one sentence that the recipient can use to explain it easily to anyone else.

ONE SENTENCE:

A new, worldwide, Thoroughbred wagering sport is starting up, Celebrities World 4-Horse Chariot Racing League, that is much more exciting than jockey Thoroughbred racing, that will build its own destination-raceway, surrounded by hotels with casinos, near Las Vegas, and can potentially become as large as current Thoroughbred racing worldwide, grossing well into the double-digit billions of dollars in due course, even a billion dollars a day.

Four-horse chariot racing teams from every nation in Europe, North America, Asia, Australia, Mexico to Argentina, and Africa, can compete in a spectacularly exciting sport, 365 nights a year. The World 4-Horse Chariot Racing League can be *the basis of the largest TV business ever.*

ALL THE TEAMS ARE SPONSORED: As in auto racing, the advertising sponsor pays all the costs of the team, the team owners keep all profits from winnings, plus fees, perhaps large, that may make for a guaranteed annual profit. *One sponsor only* per team.

Another reason to consider this business is the planned LEAGUE of LEADING FAMILIES as one of the conferences of the World 4-Horse Chariot Racing League. Currently, there is no forum where the world's leading business families can meet in casual, social circumstances. Perhaps they can meet in the League of Leading Families.

Noted in passing, Suuuper!Party! will not nominate any Presidential candidate who has not stated with clarity that he or she will sign legislation for legal, online wagering on Celebrities World 4-Horse Chariot Racing League, with the Federal Beneficial Automatic IRA Sports Wagering Trust. Ten percent of each wager goes into the wagerer's *Automatic Individual Retirement Account.* Wagering is to be limited to Debit Cards, with credit cards excluded. Winnings are taxed, the wagering handle not taxed, no way, no how. Contributions to the Automatic Individual Retirement Account are tax deductible from taxes on winnings.

Suuuper!Party!, to field candidates for all 500,000 Elective Public Offices in the U.S. (Chapter Eighteen), asserts that it is not The Purpose Of Human Activity On The Planet Earth to provide taxes to bloated, daffy, line-dancing bureaucrats. The purpose is to love your family and friends and community and nation, have some fun, and get prosperous.

A part of the plan to introduce Celebrities World 4-Horse Chariot Racing League is in double-full-page announcements in the world's major financial newspapers, in the U.S., Europe, Brazil, China, Hong Kong, India, and elsewhere.

Herewith a sample draft. To be fully illustrative it includes a bit of repetition from the previous pages, which can be skipped over.

A GREAT, NEW, UNMATCHABLE SPORTS LEAGUE IS BEING ORGANIZED

Should You Be Part of the League?
Should You Own Part or All of a Team?
Should Your Corporation Obtain League Equity?

After a temporary absence of 2,500 years, the world's most exciting entertainment is back! The World 4-IIorse Chariot Racing League revives the greatest sport of the ancient world. To fill the worldwide market for universal sports television. In modern, safe form, as family entertainment. 200 nations and social groups can compete nightly on world sports TV.

Why Four-Horse Chariot Racing?

It is extremely rare to find an entertainment and sports business that is pre-sold from motion pictures and history. Four horse chariot racing has *star quality*. Every nation is equally skilled at it. League 4-horse chariot racing can be telecast world-wide 12+ hours a day and become a great, worldwide passion.

Celebrities World 4-Horse Chariot Racing League with wagering:
• Lends itself to spirited competition among nations and cities, as well as social groups, and leading families.

• Can be telecast on worldwide television daily for hours, and has no language or cultural barriers.

• Can show in any 10 minutes of television viewing a tense drama with preparation, a beginning, a middle, an end, a resolution.

• Lends itself to pageantry, ceremony and color, and modern staging techniques including rock concert-genre lighting, power music, and power announcers, actually shouting, screaming, acting-out announcers.

• Involves grandstands and grandstand crowds, and the excitement of wagering.

• Can carry television cameras in the midst of its own pell-mell, frantic action, broadcast to giant public-screen, and worldwide television.

• Is a family entertainment enjoyed by fans from young children to senior citizens.

• Involves something as universal and perpetual, and loved, as Thoroughbred horses.

• Can have charioteer-gladiators become national and world heroes, and can spawn film and television dramas.

• Can be a major regional and national destination tourist attraction.

The Format of World 4-Horse Chariot Racing League Racing

Celebrities World 4-Horse Chariot Racing League racing can be a more compelling production than the old-style chariot racing such as seen in the motion picture *Ben-Hur*. The modern revival has a much better pre-race drama. Spectacularly beautiful chariots. And is systematically safer for charioteers and horses: There is no real weight limit on charioteer armor made of plastic and composites. The four horses are individually hitched with easy-hitches and breakaway tack on chariots with brakes. Chariot wheels are required to have suspension, independently, while yet looking like 'Ancient Roman'-appearing chariot wheels. No rubber or pneumatic tires. Chariots can have, believe it or not, gear boxes like bicycles and motorcycles or transmissions not excluding microprocessor read-outs; differentials; and fly wheels. Reason: for complexities of competition. There is no whipping of the horses.

The Significance of The Pre-Race Race

The pre-race foot race, an elaborate Le Mans start, means that the League makes use of *the countdown clock tension of modern sports.*

THE COUNTDOWN CLOCK STARTS: The Five Parts of the pre-race foot race then proceed, with fans and charioteers and pre-race race team helpers all tensely watching the count-down clock, and shouting, "Go! Go!"

The 4-horse chariot race begins when the countdown clock hits "00" *regardless of whether every team is ready.* So the leisurely, 'sipping mint juleps,' Victorian-era start of jockey Thoroughbred racing becomes a thing of the past.

The Five Parts of the Pre-race Race

Part One of the Pre-Race: At the starting gun and the count-down clock beginning, in a 'Le Mans start', the male charioteers, not yet in uniform, stripped to the waist on warm nights, *sprint on foot* towards their unhitched chariots, on the track, 200 meters ahead. Fifteen unhitched chariots.

During the 200 meter sprint, each charioteer is allowed two or a few NFL-genre bumps-and-runs against the other charioteers who are sprinting alongside. During this race, they can try to knock each other over. Tripping might be allowed if it works for the sport. This NFL-genre combat is exciting. Equally desirable, it also means that *only tall, tough, strong, fast professional athletes, with bodybuilder bodies, can be charioteers.*

Celebrities World 4-Horse Chariot Racing League is presumably a dangerous sport. However, it is considerably safer than jockey Thoroughbred racing. The charioteers are in chariots. They can and will wear Kevlar armor just as Brahma bull riders now wear.

Part Two of the Pre-Race: Upon reaching their chariots, each charioteer picks up the chariot hitch. Then the charioteers must haul their chariots 200 meters to the starting gate, hitch in one hand, running as fast as their athletic strength and speed allow. Thus, only former National Football League running position players and other first rate athletes possess the speed, strength and toughness to be charioteers. There is a 6-feet tall or even 6-foot-2 height minimum and charioteers must be able to bench press 300 or 400 pounds (137 or 181 kilograms). Thus the charioteers have action hero, Rambo-esque physiques, bare to the waist for the sprint. Every boy on the planet is going to want to be a charioteer. Girls want to be with him. The chariot will weigh in excess of 200 pounds with weights. There is nightly Women's World 4-Horse Chariot Racing League as well.

Ideal for hero worshipping youngsters worldwide and for adult fans as well.

Part Three of the Pre-Race: Simultaneously, in a breathtaking action scene, two men and two women sprinters, four sprinters for each of 15 teams racing, *60 sprinters total*, a breathtaking sight, bring up the four horses, 60 horses total, to the starting line, shortly to be hitched to the chariot when it arrives, all to the *count-down clock*. This can cause extreme tension in competitors and fans. Celebrities World 4-Horse Chariot Racing League may become *the* major world television sport.

Part Four of the Pre-Race: There is a four-by-200 meters relay race in which, for each of fifteen, 4-Horse Chariot Racing teams, men and women relay runners carry the quite large TEAM FLAG, perhaps 6-feet by 9-feet or larger, typically the sponsor's flag, and carry a FLAMING TORCH, towards the starting place. These two runners for each of 15 teams per race, hand-off the TEAM FLAG and FLAMING TORCH to two other runners, like the baton hand-off in relay races.

After two-hundred meters, a second hand-off of FLAG and TORCH occurs, for each team. This pre-race process is occurring for all 15 teams in the race. This means that there are fully 15 huge FLAGS and 15 FLAMING TORCHES moving 800 yards to the starting point. As most races may be at night, the site of 15 flaming torches being carried by 15 stressed-out runners, handed over to 15 other runners, along with the sponsor's flag, makes **perhaps the most spectacular sight in all of sports worldwide. Ever in the history of sports**.

Moreover, the 15 huge FLAGS and 15 FLAMING TORCHES are each planted in lengthy, vertical containers on either side at the rear of each chariot. This means that 15 chariots race with huge FLAGS flying and FLAMING TORCHES, a stunning and unique site in the world of sports.

Part Five of the Pre-Race: Meanwhile, at the starting point, to the countdown clock tension, to tense shouts, the horses are hitched up to the chariot, and the charioteer's armor and helmet, and huge flying cape, and huge, thigh-high boots put on, *every second counting desperately.* The clock is ticking down! Ticking with very loud, ominous, TICK-TOCKS heard on the public address system. The chariot is hitched to the 4-horses, perhaps a pipe-sleeve-and-dowel style hitch.

Television cameras a few feet above the thick of the action record this super-exciting scene. *The horse handlers are frantically shouting directions and warnings.* The horses may kick back at someone's head! The clock is nearing '00'!

Must be ready! Must be ready! Must be ready!

This all means that before the race even begins, fans will be standing and tensely shouting "Come on! Come on!"

At '00' on the clock, and an *ear-splitting clarion call on the public address*, the charioteers jump onto their chariots and race off. The teams that are ready. Any that are not ready, that are late, cause groans in the fans, especially fans who have bet on the late-to-start team.

The charioteers' armor includes clear plastic visors or clear, head-fitting covers with their 'ancient Roman Centurion' plumed helmets. This allows safe and spectacular, bring-the-crowds-to-their-feet, wheel-to-wheel 'whipping' duels, called Mano a Mano, between the male charioteers wildly lashing at each other with huge, thick, though harmless whips, 10 to 15 feet long. Thick means that the whip handle itself may be two-inches in diameter and two-feet long. The whip may be one-inch in diameter at the end. As possible, the whips will be lit from within in various colors.

At some or all races, each 4-horse chariot team may have three 'Dukes' and 'Duchesses', on horseback and, with flying cloak/capes, following the field at 100 meters back, racing around the track at a gallop. The 'Dukes' and 'Duchesses' can steady the horses post-race. They can carry the sponsor's or family's flag before the grandstand and television in review and in victory laps to standing ovations. They can carry the sponsor's or family's standard, which can be gold gilt and with tapestry. Or lighted.

Family members of both sexes, 16 and over, can be Knights, with at least one adult supervisor, 'Duke' or 'Duchess'. League 4-horse chariot racing is thus the only professional sport where family members and young people can participate on the field.

There are annual money prizes for each conference for The Most Beautiful 4-Horse Chariot Team. This means, gorgeous chariot, perhaps shiny gold. Beautiful horses. Horse vans. Truck. Gleaming silver or shiny gold truck engines. Shimmering gold or silver truck underbody. Chariot garage. Charioteer dress and armor. Cheerleader uniforms. Everything.

The World 4-Horse Chariot Racing League's modern revival of four-horse chariot racing stands to be: Sport. Spectacle. Pageantry. Peaceful outlet for national and cultural pride. A worldwide common denominator. A substantial new industry. Showing that neither victory nor defeats endure. Family fun. The fascination of equal competition between teams from large and small institutions and nations.

A current example of a successful racing sport with four hitched Thoroughbred horses, though two-in-front-of-two, is the 100-year old chuckwagon races of the Calgary Stampede and in the Western states. The Calgary Stampede chuckwagon races are far more taxing on the horses than 4-horse chariot racing (because in two-in-front-of-two horses the rear horses must do most of the pulling, and the 4-wheels chuckwagon weighs a very heavy 1,350 pounds plus the two-fisted cowboy).

The Heart Of The Sport

What the long ball is to baseball,

What collision contact, and the long pass, are to football,

What the slam dunk and battling below the basket is to basketball,

What bodychecking and fighting is to hockey,

The wild wheel-to-wheel, Mano a Mano 'whipping' duels all over the track are to 4-horse chariot racing. (Wearing football, hockey-genre and Iron Man armor and face visors, the charioteers cannot ordinarily be hurt.)

It is spectacularly exciting. Fan emotions can become wild as favorite teams and charioteers - often from their own nation, state, province, city, social group (for examples, Indians of Peru!, American Indian Warrior!) alumni group, fraternity, corporation, leading family battle it out all over the track.

In their Seven League boots that rise above the knee, helmets with plumes, the charioteers, standing 6-feet-2 to 6-feet-6 in any case, will stand seven feet to seven-and a half feet tall. They will be *enormous*. It will be like watching huge Shaquille O'Neills in pell-mell racing chariots and whipping each other.

As in auto racing, there can be celebrity charioteers in an occasional race-for-fun: athlete celebrities from other sports. Motion picture and TV celebrities. Music celebrities.

THE HEART OF THE SPORT may for many fans be the hard-to-articulate compelling, magnetic, thrilling nature of 4-horse chariot racing. "There is just something about it."

It is magnificent and compelling.

The World Women's 4-Horse Chariot Racing League World 4-Horse Chariot Racing League can be the only field sport that has women athletes playing on the same field as the men athletes on the same night. Except for the MAiNGlobal Football/Soccer League. Fun Disruptor Chapter Fifteen.

There is no extra cost or logistics by this format. When a 4-horse chariot team finds itself seeded into the Tenth Race on any night, it must use a woman charioteer. The men's league has a height minimum. It may be 6-feet-2. The women's league may have a height minimum. It may be 5-feet-10. Maybe 6-feet!

Women can be great fans of this sport as well as men.

Women fans also can enjoy watching the heroic male charioteers. And the beautiful horses not only when racing but in back-of-the-track interviews next to the horses.

The women charioteers will not use the whipping duels (to avoid the roller derby and women's mud wrestling set in both fans and athletes) and their pre-race foot race may or may not include hauling the chariot. Perhaps, sprinting 200 meters to the already-hitched chariot.

What Makes Up This Televised League?

Team development groups. Sports television networks. National media companies. Companies that may want to participate in the consortium of Chariots Entertainment Television, to be a separate company, and IPO, with its 24 hours a day of worldwide sports television. Sports marketers. Manufacturers licensing. Sports and entertainment celebrities. Potential team sponsors. Large professional athletes interested in careers as charioteer-gladiators or team managers. Thoroughbred horse trainers.

Individuals and private groups that may not now be engaged in any sport at all can enter 4-horse chariot teams, with a sponsor to pay costs for fielding and operating the team, and perhaps a guaranteed profit.

Each individual or group that intends to enter a team constitutes a Team Development Group, a League member, and a delegate to the League. The shape and development of the World 4-Horse Chariot Racing League will be decided in some continuing measure by the members, including your team, as in the other sports leagues. Each board member of your team can communicate at will with any or all of the others daily on the League's private Intranet forums. You may serve on a League committee. Your team is an independent corporation run by you as you see fit, like having a team on an auto racing circuit.

To maintain an accessible cost structure, there can always be low-cost claiming race levels in each conference. Yet any team may be eligible to get into the annual Universe Cup Tournament and Judgment Day. Each team may be able to protect some horses sometimes from being claimed. The low-cost structure may allow sponsors with modest national advertising budgets to sponsor a team and to obtain national and even worldwide television at reasonable cost.

Handicapping for parity will be by lead weights under the chariot floor. And by spectacular, oblique-line staggered starts. Although the planned Flat-side-Infinite Loop race track, if there is a figure-8 intersection, in front of the grandstands, nullifies some rail-position advantage. The team next to the rail become the team farthest from the rail.

As a true world League, all the teams, racetracks, television and suppliers can meet annually in one world garden spot or another to decide World 4-Horse Chariot Racing League policies and plans. Here and on the League site, every nation, team, sponsor, and other participant speaks and proposes *directly* to all the other teams and nations rather than having to go through League headquarters.

The Annual Universe Cup Tournament

All this leads to the annual The Universe Cup Tournament, a perhaps eight summer weekends tournament, to be watched by two billion people or more as *The World's Pre-Eminent Annual Sporting Event.*

The final day of The Universe Cup Tournament, known dramatically as Judgment Day, decides *the* one and only Champion of All Champions, the Global Super Champion team.

The champion charioteer is Emperor Caesar for a Year. "He Bestrides the World Like a Colossus", (from Shakespeare's Julius Caesar), with the greatest athletic fame ever, much greater than a heavyweight boxing champion.

In Great Global Victory, your team receives the Great Gold Chalice Cup. Four feet high, worth seven-figures.

The winner of the Women's League is Empress of the World for a Year.

In due course, there may be eight-figure purses. History will absolve us.

Each team can have its fan clubs. Its flag. Its banners. Its cheers. Its T-shirts. Its charioteer hero. Its web site that sells team-branded merchandise. Its band. Its restaurants and lounges. Its section at the race track. For advertising and sports marketing sponsors, this can mean squadrons of fans enjoying themselves by carrying sponsor posters and flags and shouting the sponsor's name. On worldwide television.

During each race day, the announcer will call for every fan to stand and applaud the sponsors who have the courage to sponsor a team even though they cannot know whether it might come in last. Each night there will be a 'Courage Cup' awarded with standing applause to the team that finishes slowest, to be a tradition like the seventh inning stretch. Good-bye boring win, place, show. Hello Triumph, Victory, Winner.

What if 100 individuals and groups in, say, New York City, want to enter a 4-horse chariot team flying the Big Apple flag? The teams can choose a local geographic suffix. For example: 'New York City, Staten Island'. 'New York City, East Side'. 'Great Kings County Brooklyn'. 'New York City, Forest Hills'. 'Harlem'. 'New York, Chinatown.' In the Universe Cup Tournament heats, the New York City teams can race for the glory and potential prize money of representing New York City in the Universe Cup Tournament, Cities League.

Team names must be League approved and fit the family atmosphere yet can be spiritedly competitive and boastful in good spirits. Team names cannot be private codes, which for some weird reason Thoroughbred horse racing allows. The Kentucky Derby winner in 2013 was named Orb. Wha?

Examples of team names are such as, The Roman Empire! – The Empire State – Harlem Globemasters – Ohio Express – The Rising Sun – The Middle Kingdom – Japanese Bullet Train – New York Italians – Italian Stallions – Harlem

On My Mind – Brooklyn Guys – Chinatown Express – Shanghai Story – Brazilian Bossa Nova – The Royal Canadian Mounted Police – The Teamsters Union – Bombay Spice – Russian ICBM – The British Bulldog – French Superiority – Mexican Conquista – Egyptian Pharaohs – Boston Irish – Argentine Horsemen – Germany Over All! – Italy the Greatest – South Africa! – Bengal Tigers – The Arab Horsemen – Seoul Korea – My Heart in San Francisco – The [Your Name] Family Team – Take the A Train to Harlem – Motion Picture Producers – Honest Hollywood Talent Agents – Australian Expeditionary Force – Team AFL-CIO – Rio Carnivale – Favela People of Rio! – New York Cabbies! – Santiago! Chile – Caesar's Rome – China SuperPower – Swedish Blondes – Social Media – People of Pakistan – African American Colossus – Nigerian Man Power – Wall Street Traders – Singaporean! – The Taiwan Dragon – The Prince of Monaco – Mexico Aztecs – Malaysian Twin Towers – The Sioux Tribe – Guatemalan Indian People – Apache Warriors – Russia Our Russia! – Guangdong Province Warriors – Hong Kong Trader – USA USA! – Greatness of Britain – Rule Brittania! – Indonesia Forever – Japanese Imperial Team – Wall Street Rich Guys – Casablanca – The Mongol Invasion – Ireland Triumphant – The [Your Company] Team – The Long Island Rail Road – The Young Turks – Bangkok Kick Racer – Ghengis Khan Warriors – Manhattan Transfer – Spirit of St. Louis – The Calgary Stampede – Pacific Coast Highway – Toronto Titan – The Chicago Loop – Pride of Peru – Indian People of Peru! – Ben-Hur – O Israel! – Swiss Precision – Bengal Lancers – Thriller from Manila – The Zulu Tribe – Big Tokyo, Los Angeles – The Trans-Siberian Express – Koreatown L.A.! – The American Eagle – The Black Stallions – Beijing We Love You! – Japanese American! – The Polish Cavalry Charge – Rich Nigerian Prince – Barcelona – The Spanish Inquisition – Russian Cossacks – Colossus Of India – Texas Cowboys – South Central L.A.! – The

Maltese Falcon – The Bronx is Up! – Cubans de Miami – Great Great Africa.

There might be some carefully managed, League-supervised teams inspired by race, with each team's board of directors pointedly seen in photos to include persons of various races. The Great Black Race. The Great Chinese Race. The Great Korean Race. Etcetera. This is the cardiac arrest League.

Among those that can suitably enter teams are entertainers and music groups and companies. Power music is to be played at the grandstand and on television during 4-horse chariot racing. Therefore there is a great opportunity for music groups to sponsor a 4-horse chariot team.

A motion picture studio can name and theme its team after a film release each year for inexpensive worldwide publicity.

Motion picture producers: the League has an action-heroes screenplay about modern, league 4-horse chariot racing by an Academy-nominated screenwriter.

The Greatest Advertising Vehicle Ever

There is no greater, more spectacular advertising vehicle in or outside of sports than a 4-horse chariot team. Yet chariots are very cheap in contrast to race cars where a typical sponsor can afford only a decal. To be compared with the sewn patch on athlete's uniform or the decal of auto racing, each and all of the following bear your sponsor's colors and logo: **1.** A large flag, perhaps six-by-nine feet, flying on the aerial of the chariot. **2.** Your heroic charioteer's six foot long flying cape. **3.** The chariot itself designed and built from the ground up imaginatively to show your sponsor. For example a watch company could affix a watch on each wheel spoke to show the punishment their watches can take. A clear plastic chariot can be filled with soda pop or auto oil. Chariots can be lit by a number of car batteries, thus allowing lighted, even blinking advertising, to be compared to the dull, little decal in auto racing, which is a great sport. **4.** The Formula I-style 'spoiler', chest high to prevent horses from running into the back of the chariot in front of them, can carry major signage as in auto racing. **5.** The charioteer's chest armor can feature your company's logo, like the Superman 'S'. **6.** The charioteer's forearm armor, **7.** Gigantic, Seven League boots, **8.** Helmet and plumes. **9.** The five mandatory video broadcast cameras on the chariot can be partly pointed at the sponsor's logo. **10.** Plus 'Knights' following the field with large, sponsors' banners flying.

While your 4-horse team walks and parades on the track before and after races, the horses can have **11.** Mane-to-tail blankets that feature your sponsor's logo. Back-of-the-track interviews can feature, **12.** a background *film commercial on a movie-size screen with sound*. Other interviews can include **13.** a background *wall-size sign* held up by a cherry-picker. **14.** Mascot and cheerleaders, **15.** Cheerleaders wearing your logos and colors, and **16.** Freedom to give out promotions at raceways.

There is no sports advertising that begins to compare.

Sponsors can also have dedicated pavilions at the front-forward 'back of the track'. The trams stop at your pavilion. Show things, sell stuff, give away stuff.

Each chariot is required to have mandatory deep bas-reliefs or equivalent wind resistance. Aerodynamic, low wind resistance chariots are not allowed. Boring.

The chariots' lighting by automobile batteries can also include, if it works for the fans, lighting *underneath the chariot and shining directly down on the track* (an idea borrowed from the peculiar practice in Florida of some automobiles having lighting underneath focused on the road below, so they look like space ships).

Advertisers and Team Sponsors

Advertisers and team sponsors can sit on the World 4-Horse Chariot Racing League Committee of Advertisers and Sponsors Association and make decisions.

Same-industry sponsors can be in different conferences and races.

Should You Form A Team Development Group?

Individuals can enter teams. As can groups. Team groups can be 2 to 25 persons or more. A group of business people, CPA's, attorneys and other professionals, a group of friends, others are suitable. You might want to meet monthly for lunch to review the team business. This may be a fun business but it is very much a business. Your team is a permanent business. It may become a thoroughly profitable business year after year indefinitely. For purely speculative example, a team that chooses a good name, for example, USA! USA!, and a sponsor and great logo and wins only its share of races might return a substantial annual profit indefinitely and come to be worth some millions of dollars, perhaps much more with a major sponsor.

Teams, and team numerical position in the first 1,000 Team Development Group slots, can be bought and sold to League-acceptable parties. Acceptability includes later passing an F.B.I. check in regard to any connection to unsavory persons.

The potentially valuable, in our view, placement on the numerical list runs from WCRL# 0001 to WCRL# 1,000.

One thousand teams may seem like a lot. Yet, Thoroughbred horse racing meets often have over 1,000 horses. Thoroughbred horses can typically race only once every two weeks. One thousand teams is only an average of ten teams from 100 nations.

For reference, there are hundreds of sponsors of auto racing in America. Sponsoring a single race can cost $500,000.00.

Whether the team is to be entered by an individual or group or sponsor, each Team Development Group that forms to enter a 4-horse chariot team must have an attorney on its board of directors in due course. An accountant. Each team needs to obtain one or more board members, or outsource to consultants in marketing and manufacturer's licensing for your team's individual logos and trademarks and images.

The League is to go forward as a juggernaut, the greatest world sports league ever. The day-by-day team management can be done by a full-time executive. *Teams may prefer a sponsor-paid fee to a sports marketer to obtain the team sponsor.*

A business plan for your 4-horse chariot team: The one-only commercial sponsor pays all of the expenses of your team, including your management expenses, and your League fee expenses retroactively, and may pay a profit before the first race is run each year. The team owners keep the winnings. The sponsor obtains great national and worldwide advertising. In this arrangement, the team owners supposedly would lose nothing and might have considerable profits, while having a good deal of enjoyment.

A League 4-horse chariot racing team is to be a permanent corporation and, if successful, profitable year after year, perhaps decade after decade. And with success, having beaten the learning-curve, a person or group may be able to field other teams. This is a sports league in which you can own more than one team, the commissioner approving. An IPO may become possible for your team. And for a number of teams together.

Your team's operators can, should, and need to make use of the League's private Intranet forums. Information and tips and documents on any area of knowledge can be exchanged daily, seven days a week worldwide. All the teams' attorneys, C.P.A.'s and other executives have their own departments online, downloading non-proprietary documents and information worldwide, and talking to each other.

Online on the League site you can weigh-in daily with your views. 'Our team thinks that....'

Like the National Football League and other leagues, each team may be able to serve on various committees: Television. Syndication. Official League Sponsors. Expansion. Rules. Licensing. Scheduling. Liaison with investment banking firms, and so on.

You can keep in touch daily at will with your team organizer/coach/trainer man or woman and charioteers at the race track by Skype. Your team's chariot can have a smartphone. Talk to your heroic charioteer pre-race and post-race. If he is in a good mood.

Each chariot carries fully five video-cameras. Facing front. Facing left. Facing right. Facing rear. And facing upwards on your charioteer as he heroically engages in Mano a Mano whipping duels, often against ferocious brutes, with such names as The Nigerian Monster and The Brazilian Killer, on both sides of his chariot. Each video-camera can be telecast worldwide, and to the home nation.

Each team has access to the League president and the League commissioner. And has 24 hour access to its headquarters-paid Team Account Executive at the League headquarters, in Nevada or Florida for tax reasons. The League site is like a daily convention. The site will include a daily-updated Suppliers Pages of suppliers of goods and services worldwide: chariot makers, sports marketers, Thoroughbred horse breeders, makers of designer tack in all colors, whip makers, uniform makers, team managers, horse trainers, charioteers, pre-race sprinters, want ads, horse feed, veterinarians, heroic stall muckers, even more heroic horse manure collectors, worldwide transporters, and everything under the sun.

At the beginning of the League, the team-development groups will have a step-by-step, date-by-date, simultaneous-development schedule. 'By such and such a date must have commissioned your chariot....' This schedule is to be something of a consensus schedule. To protect each team, any that fall behind must exchange places on the waiting-list.

The charioteers must be world class athletes, for the reasons noted.

There is to be a World Charioteers Guild. As a model for young people, charioteers are not allowed to nurse real-actual grudges and must be willing to shake hands on television at any time with any other charioteer. Same with owners.

However, there may well be League-dramatized and directed "grudges" and "pushing and shoving fights" that require The Huge Guards to "break-up".

For example, the public address suddenly shouts, "Japanese Bullet Train's Isoroku Yamamoto jumps USA! USA! Team's Monster-from-Montana! They are really going at it!" The Huge Guards run over to break-it-up. Calm down, boys. All is shown on a huge, center-hung, diamond-vision screen, as in Cowboys Stadium. The fans will love their two-fisted heroes defending Truth and Justice.

As a true world league, all the charioteers from every nation and social group will train together. The plan is to build a very large World League Charioteers Training Center next to O BEHOLD! O The World's Great Raceway!, outside Las Vegas. The charioteers will be trained in handling four horses, horse safety, chariot handling, Mano and Mano whipping duels, rules, and duties of relationship to the fans, ages five to ninety-five. There will also be Hollywood stunt men and directors showing how to stage "pushing and shoving fights" and NFL-genre "gang tackles" and other staged confrontations.

The charioteers must evidence good sportsmanship, stay for autographs signing and photos with the fans, and be "visibly good to their mothers and wives". There is to be a special section of O Behold! for moms and dads and other family, to cheer on their heroic sons, and daughters who are women charioteers or sprinters and horse handlers in the pre-race race. A charioteer in any trouble at all with the law is out of the League.

Each and every charioteer must make a video saying, "A Real Man will not raise his hand to a woman. Any of you men out there who have been hitting the woman in your life, I want you to turn to her and apologize. Because no Real Man hits a woman. If you want to punch something, go outside and hit a tree. *Love Her.*" Then, once a week or so, the Winning Charioteer for that week will make the noted worldwide announcement.

There has never been anything like it, Anywhere, Anytime.

How Specifically To Participate In Formation of a Team Development Group

Decide whether you wish to be a lead team-organizer or other active participant or a less active part owner of a team. A team group can be organized by one man or woman, or by two or a few persons.

The League web site, when built, can act as Communications Central to assist you in forming or joining a group in your area by putting you in touch with other interested men and women in your area.

A Free Market League: The League intends to be something of a free market League, not a bureaucratic office with supplicants supplicating. Perhaps powerful, vigorous continent-conferences may develop in time. As in government, bureaucrats in the private sector do not know that they do not know. No one knows whether there should be 1,000 or 1,500 teams, or hours of sports on TV, or how many Italian restaurants there should be in America.

But Will Your Team Make Money?

As in other sports leagues, the League intends to be structured from the beginning so that teams that do not win their share of races might be profitable. Like the NFL. Might. Each team wants its one-only sponsor to pay all expenses, plus provide a profit, win or lose.

Bear in mind, there will be no racing until the Celebrities World 4-Horse Chariot Racing League new-built **O BEHOLD! O The World's Great Raceway!** near Las Vegas has been built. Team Development Groups will not be proceeding forward with building chariots and hiring charioteers until O Behold is within sight of being open, if it is built. The current plan: constructed sixteen hours a day, seven days a week.

The plan is that each team may stand to make money from purses, television, Official League Sponsors, League merchandise licensing, your own team merchandise licensing of your logos, and so on. The League will not succeed and grow in the U.S. and abroad unless most teams profit, or at least break even each year.

Of course, no guarantees at all should be construed here. You team can lose money with no recourse. It is 100% owned and operated by you or your group. Your team can go bankrupt, as with any business. Individual World 4-Horse Chariot Racing League teams or a group of teams can have an IPO.

In the League's view, your sponsor should be expected to pay to you the amount that each team investor may have paid, that these expenses are recouped.

As in other sports leagues, each team is to participate in the television, sponsorship and licensing and other revenue, if any. To speculate blue sky, if nine figures were divided among 1,000 teams, this would be six-figures per team. Ten figures divided among 1,000 teams is seven-figures per team. Plus your sponsor fees. Plus individual team merchandise licensing. There may be ten figures to be divided.

The League intends to share a fixed percentage of television and licensing revenues with racing teams. Of course again, no guarantees of any revenue should be construed here. The League does not know.

The League Conferences

Currently, seven conferences are tentatively planned. Each year can include entries from all of the seven: 1. Nations. 2. Cities. 3. States and provinces. 4. Sports and Entertainment Celebrities, individually or a group of friends. 5. Corporations. 6. League of Leading Families. 7. Fraternities and University Alumni teams from major universities worldwide (except Yale because Yale alumni would be scared of being creamed by Harvard).

As The World 4-Horse Chariot Racing League is to be a true world league, there might be, in time, Celebrities World 4-Horse Chariot Racing League-Europe, Celebrities World 4-Horse Chariot Racing League-Asia, Celebrities World 4-Horse Chariot Racing League-Latin America, Celebrities World 4-Horse Chariot Racing League-Africa, each with their own headquarters. *All of these now merely virtual Leagues can field teams and compete interleague at the first raceway, O Behold!.*

The League of Leading Families

There is to be a league conference composed of entries by leading families of the world. There can be few better common endeavors for a family than to have a family 4-horse chariot team in The World 4-Horse Chariot Racing League.

Like the other conferences, the League of Leading Families can have various claiming race structures, thus allowing inexpensive 4-horse chariot teams. As well as higher claiming when desired. A team may be sponsored by a corporation connected to the family.

These teams can still have advertising sponsors, just as some NASCAR teams have nationally prominent owners operating them, and also a group of advertiser sponsors. Many NASCAR teams maintain their own web sites that feature compelling content, and merchandise for sale.

A Leading Family team can be anywhere from entirely organized and operated by one or more family members to organized and trained by a current racing stable for a family. A group of families can enter a team together.

Leading Family teams can include fan clubs. Limited partnerships.

As in each League conference, the League of Leading Families can have its own League site section, and club rules. Entry may become by recommendation only.

Each family can develop its own crests and flags.

The League of Leading Families is to be, like the other conferences, a true world League from the beginning. Leading families of the world from Brazil to Hong Kong, from Britain to Kuwait, France to Japan, from Canada to Chile, from Ireland to Italy to Israel to India, from Australia to Zimbabwe, from

Zambia to New Zealand and the Philippines and China and Singapore are invited to take up the great challenge and compete
for incandescent and imperishable world glory by entering a
4-horse chariot team in Celebrities World 4-Horse Chariot Racing League and the annual Universe Cup Tournament watched
by '2 billion' people. One hundred years from now your victory
will be re-shown worldwide, at the annual Universe Cup, to
be seen by your great, great grandchildren. Like Bobby Jones'
Masters victories.

The League of Leading Families members or their corporation must hold a minimum of one-third of the equity in their
entry. Class B stock, fine. A team can issue public stock.

*The family aura of the League of Leading Families makes a
major reason for corporate sponsorship of teams in the various conferences.*

ONE OF THE LARGER BUSINESS SECTORS?: The League
of Leading Families also positions a family in a whole new
industry that worldwide may become as large as the *entire*
popular music business or the *entire* worldwide motion picture
business, and come to be on television for 8-to-24 hours a day
worldwide.

World 4-Horse Chariot Racing League racing may be able
to become a strong growth industry: Hong Kong with 6 million people, does equal to the entire U.S. in Thoroughbred pari-
mutuel wagering per annum. League 4-horse chariot racing
might become one of the larger entertainment businesses on
earth.

The No-Limits League

Demand arising, there may be a no-limits League, a locomotive for all teams. The No-Limits League will use the name

Global Giants League. Claiming-race amounts may proceed upwards year by year as decided by a simple majority of the teams in Global Giants League, and the powerful commissioner. For example in thousands of dollars claiming per horse: 50, 100, 250, 500, 1,000, perhaps No Limit/No Claiming. At the Universe Cup Tournament, the Global Giants League can race for The 1,000 Year Immortals Cup.

Each of the Global Giants League teams may be owned by a world's leading family and/or by a public corporation.

Race Tracks

Race tracks, called Raceways in Celebrities World 4-Horse Chariot Racing League parlance, might come to be built in more than one nation in time. Each with perhaps 365 days of worldwide televised League 4-horse chariot racing. Each raceway needs to be a world-destination raceway, with a very wide track, to accommodate 60 horses side-by-side, famously spacious, immense stable and clean, inviting, chariot garages area, and a tram or theme park train to take fans and tourists around the raceway, including the exciting back-of-the-track where all the charioteers and chariot teams are seen to be thrillingly busy, with horses having horse shoes put on, red hot metal being pulled from blazing furnaces, sledgehammers hitting anvils, and so on. Hero charioteers wave to their fans.

The raceway track, where the horses run, needs to be soft or able to be made soft with the currently used layer of ground-up rubber tires and such. The League intends to be a good citizen of the Thoroughbred industry and can give first hiring notice to the usual Thoroughbred people. Except, alas, jockeys, or at least those jockeys who are under 6-foot-2 in height and under 240 pounds in weight.

A participating nation can place an executive in the League world headquarters.

Wagering: worldwide television would allow wagering by Internet, where legal. The League's *Beneficial Automatic Individual Retirement Account* has been noted, in which 10% of each and every wager goes into the individual wagerer's IRA. This feature may be well-liked by legislators.

Theme Park Opportunity

Celebrities World 4-Horse Chariot Racing League raceways must be dedicated, destination raceways. They need to be designed for family visits and enjoyment and be to old-style race tracks as Disney World is to the old sawdust carnivals. The race track itself will be in the revolutionary, trade dress, Flat-side-Infinite Loop Raceway shape. This shape gives maximum crowd viewing pleasure and 'fighting for the rail position' excitement. In the Flat-side-Infinite Loop shape race track, with grandstands at the flat-side, the grandstand fans see closely, each race, fifteen 4-horse chariot racing teams thunder by, and *at*, and *from,* them 3 or 4 separate times, 45-60 times per 15-race day. There may be a figure-8 intersection. No binoculars needed as in Thoroughbred horse racing's old-fashioned oval.

Each thundering pass by, with the heroic charioteers whipping wildly at each other in Mano a Mano dueling, may bring 200,000 shouting fans to their feet. It is equivalent to the home run or long pass touchdown, yet much more exciting. Some Asian race tracks get crowds as large as 265,000. The Indianapolis 500 has a seating capacity of 257,000. The Kentucky Derby gets attendance of 163,000, once a year, not 365 days a year.

Sample themes: The Forum of the 12 Caesars Raceway. Ben-Hur Raceway. The Raceway of the 100 Nations. Asia's World Tourist Raceway. Rio's World Raceway Park. Australia's 100 Nations Raceway. The World Show of Shows Raceway.

O Behold! and any other destination raceway park that come to be built, if others do, can have two, three or four separated super-entrances, each like the Arc de Triomphe, 164 feet high, 148 feet wide, and each featuring the name of a different film studio. Or gaming resort. Or Fortune 500 corporation. Or network sports channel. Or a resort/gaming group. Or Las Vegas hotel-resort.

At O! Behold!, we want huge bronze statues, peraps thirty feet/ten meters high, of four horses and chariot and charioteer, like the very stylized, glorious four horses and chariot at Versailles. Google, Apollo Fountain at Versailles. Maybe photos can be taken of fans seated atop the great horses at O! Behold!.

A World Chariots Raceway tour around the park can feature permanent *Sponsor Pavilions*. Individual team tourist attractions. A ring of garden restaurant patios in a huge square. The headquarters of the national teams can fly their flag high and feature each nation's architecture, style, and glory with a national visitor's center on '5 Continents/100 Nations Square'.

At 15 races a day, 225 teams racing each day, each national team may race more than once a week, to the heartfelt, top-lung passions of visiting nationals for their team and Hero Charioteer.

Motion picture stars' teams and World Leading Families' teams can have *permanent headquarters with retail store for visitors*. Eatertainment restaurants. The small-gauge railway can take visitors through the actual and fantastical/historic 4-horse chariot racing/theme park back lot. 'See the drama of Caesar's Rome.' Hollywood talent agencies, always well-loved, can be League participants variously.

One or a few major investors, real-estate firms, and/or race tracks, and/or resorts could put together a major "World Chariot Racing Raceway" project after seeing how O BEHOLD! O The World's Great Raceway! works out.

Individual team advertiser sponsors may participate in a raceway/theme park project, for both financial and advertising benefits.

Thousands of Jobs for a Nation or U.S. State

A Celebrities World 4-Horse Chariot Racing League World Raceway complex can mean thousands of jobs directly and, by being a destination attraction, thousands of jobs in the surrounding tourist industry.

Chariots Licensing Properties Corporation

World League 4-Horse Chariot Racing may provide the largest sports and collectibles licensing opportunities in sports history. It stands to be the first truly worldwide sports League.

Celebrities World 4-Horse Chariot Racing League four-color logos, variously with men and women charioteers, stand alone. They invoke action, triumph, glory, confidence, power, an ancient provenance, a sport of unmatched prestige, and the ageless icon of horses: the basis of a 100-year product. The horses can be gloriously stylized, like the Apollo Fountain Horses at Versailles. Licensing opportunities are in men's and women's apparel including casual wear, sportswear lines and a major jeans line. Consumables. T-shirts. Collectible cards. Jewelry and other accessories.

Merchandise licensing often provides the second major source of revenue to sports leagues. Licensees bear the risk.

For video games that use film sources, 4-horse can provide ever changing, spectacular, unique videogame programming. Toys including chariots for both tots and pre-teens. Television cartoons. Comics. Posters. Bronzes. Silver plates. Commemorative coins.

The Association of 4-Horse Chariot Racing Licensees can help to make policy.

League 4-horse chariot racing merchandise licensing may become a large business. It might be that Celebrities World 4-Horse Chariot Racing League merchandise licensing can be larger than all of the other professional sports league licensing combined. It is Huge Hero Charioteer-Gladiators versus skinny guys-in-short-pants sports and guys in slow-moving sports.

Advantages for Sports Marketers

League 4-horse chariot racing constitutes the greatest sports marketing opportunity ever. It can include entries from, and television to, dozens of nations. It can be like World Cup soccer 12 months a year, a great world passion.

In addition to entering a 4-horse chariot racing team, there are levels of sports marketing sponsorship: Official Sponsor. Sponsor of a race meet. A race day. An individual race. Presenting sponsor. Participating sponsor.

In all the world of sports sponsorship, there is nothing that can remotely compare to the spectacular effect of a Celebrities World 4-Horse Chariot Racing League team.

There is direct sponsorship. For example, 'The [Name of Product] Team. There is indirect sponsorship. For example, 'Team USA USA', Sponsored by [Name of Sponsor].'

How World League 4-Horse Chariot Racing Can Fill a Worldwide Television Sports Network

Just one raceway venue can give say, 8 hours a day of spectacularly exciting racing counting time for commercials and promos, 15 races a day, 225 teams racing every day. And perhaps twice that if an O Behold raceway in Las Vegas runs 16 or more hours a day. This is enough to anchor and fill a branded TV channel worldwide.

As previously done in Asian satellite television, tens of thousands of minutes of advertising may be sold prior to launch. The programming might be given to sports network channels in return for a split of advertising revenues.

How Your Sponsor Can Get 4-to-8+ Hours a Year on Worldwide Television

Say that your sponsored team races only twice per month (and you may race once a week). Counting pre-race color, the five parts of the pre-race race to countdown clock tension, the race and post-race as 10 minutes multiplied by 24 races a year is 240 minutes on television a year. That is, *four hours annually on worldwide television for your sponsor*. It is Eight Hours Annually on worldwide television from a weekly race for each team. More if a team sometimes races twice a week. How much do television sponsors pay currently for eight hours on compelling worldwide television?

These numbers do not count leisurely interviews after the race and at your team's very inviting, open 'garage' at the back-of-the-track. Pre-race, race, and post-race color can emphasize home-nation sponsored teams, as each nation does in Olympic Games broadcasts.

Some individuals may watch Celebrities World 4-Horse Chariot Racing League for hours a day, on television, tablets, Amazon Kindles, smartphones, with friends at lunch, at work when the boss is not looking, and after work and on weekends.

In public places currently, everyone seems to be looking at their screen. This viewing may come often to be Celebrities World 4-Horse Chariot Racing League. What other purpose in life can there be?

Smartphone companies are now developing fold-out, roll-out screens. This could mean that in a bar or restaurant, everyone is looking at World 4-Horse Chariot Racing League racing on, say, a horizontal 6-inch by 10-inch, high-definition screen.

Celebrities World 4-Horse Chariot Racing League is the *sole television opportunity in history* that can offer, if O Behold Raceway in Las Vegas were open and racing 24 hours a day, like Las Vegas, 24 hours a day of universal-culture, breathlessly exciting television with teams from 200 nations and social groups with millions of emotional fans, literally flying national flags on the chariots' aerials. Thus a major media corporation or media consortium *can enter worldwide telecasting with a brand new, 24 hours worldwide, branded television channel.*

Here is *shouting-in-the-living room* television. In 150 and more nations.

Here is *pandemonium, screaming in the sports bar television* as National Heroes with body-builder physiques, *standing 7-foot-6* with boots and helmets with plumes, thunder wheel-to-wheel down the track fighting heroically for national and team glory and frantically, wildly 'whipping' at and bravely enduring the Mano a Mano 'whipping' from dastardly challengers on both sides of him. To shouting and screaming, acting-out, by pairs of power announcers. To electrifying, booming pop music on television. People from 5 to 95 on 5 continents can be daily devoted fans.

Herein is a Once-in-a-Century opportunity for a worldwide television network with universal common denominators.

Should You, Your Group, Corporation Or Family Become Involved In League 4-Horse Chariot Racing?

Other Potential Advantages for Team Development Groups

Team Executive Action: Your Team Development Group can develop a great logo and sell merchandise with your logo and the League logos, perhaps before your team or the League are underway. An entrepreneur can own one team and organize and run one or more other teams.

An event that might increase the value of an early-purchased Team Racing Medallion WCRL# 0001 to WCRL# 1,000: The League hiring of a major, nationally known, Fortune 500-genre chief executive officer, if this happens.

It might prove to be of financial advantage to have the lower, early Team Medallion Number in WCRL# 0001 up to WCRL# 1,000. Some Team Racing Medallions may be sold by owners to acceptable parties before racing begins, if it does.

The League Commissioner reserves the right to exclude persons found arbitrarily by the League to be unpleasant, or unsuitable for a wagering sport according to League view. Or who flunk F.B.I.-clearance. Alas, we had to turn down Vinny the Chin. Vinny flunked. He wept. Sorry, Vinny!

Owning a League 4-horse chariot team is an ideal way for celebrities to keep their name before the public weekly on television.

League 4-horse chariot racing may be the coming world television passion and common denominator of daily conversation worldwide.

Celebrities World 4-Horse Chariot Racing League Management Corporation

Celebrities World 4-Horse Chariot Racing League Management Corporation may manage venues worldwide, if they are built. For example, Disney Co. receives a major part of its profits from managing Disney parks that are built with 'other people's money'.

In the future, destination "Raceways" in partnerships with resort, film studios and gaming corporations, **World 4-Horse Chariot Race Track Management Corporation** might be able to generate substantial profits, if built.

Talent agencies themselves can become equity owners of Celebrities World 4-Horse Chariot Racing League.

Chariots as a Fashion/Lifestyle Trademark

Some of the most successful trademarks are horse-based. Reason: horses don't go out of fashion. They are perpetual. Thus, Ralph Lauren/Polo, Gucci, Hermes, Ferrari are some well-known equine fashion/lifestyle trademarks. None so far use greatly stylized horses such as seen at Versailles. The League does. These are us.

Chariots/ The Neighborhood Pub/Club/Sports Bar

Some bar chains in Britain number in the thousands. Chariots/The Neighborhood Pub/Club/Sports Bar is meant to become a franchise with as many establishments as the largest, worldwide restaurants, such as McDonald's and Starbucks, two superb chains. This is The Mission Statement.

CHARIOTS is to be a large, attractive, warm, sports bar. Unexpectedly, it to be fairly dark, a "dark bar", with muted, often indirect lighting, and opaque windows. This is in sharp contrast to the super-brightness-and-pink-vinyl-and-large-windows look of many other restaurant chains. Each booth and table will also include its own dimmer. Good for romance.

Another signature of each Chariots: a sylvan, garden court-yard part of the restaurant.

For World 4-Horse Chariot Racing League racing, Chariots sports bars with two or three rooms might work: one room for shouting, even screaming young men and women during races, seen on 'ten' high definition screens, with one wall-size screen. A second room for couples who enjoy a Thoroughbred sport but not pandemonium and table pounding by young males. This can also be a business-lunch place.

Another Reason to Take an Interest In The World 4-Horse Chariot Racing League and its Chariots Entertainment Television

This is a Sports Business that stands to attract nation-ally prominent and world prominent wealthy people as Team Owners.

Thoroughbred racing has been called the 'sport of kings'. Four-horse is *the* classic sport. It is human heroes, the charioteers.

There stands to be a tremendous amount of excitement for the individuals who own a team that is seen weekly on world-wide television by persons in 196 nations.

It is possible that a number of the world's richest individuals will field teams.

Animal Care

Thoroughbred horses are pampered 24 hours a day by peo-ple who go into the business because they love animals. Race horses love to run. They race only a few minutes every two weeks. There is no whipping of the horses.

The League will use elaborate breakaway tack for horse safety.

All horses will have a pre-race health check, including X-rays of legs, conducted by independent veterinarians who do not work for the teams.

Many of today's graduates of equine colleges are young women who visibly love the horses under their care. As a *League signature*, they will daily be shown on television caring for the horses, and present a different picture than big, tough-looking charioteers might.

Additionally, the League will invite the Society for the Prevention of Cruelty to Animals to have free space and a building at the 'back of the track' horse barns area.

To discourage use of not clearly ready-to-race Thoroughbred horses, when a horse breaks down on the track, the team must pay to the League, within 72 hours, *twice* or *three times* what the team paid for the horse. The veterinarian may be fined four figures.

Wild Mano a Mano Duels Between Charioteer Athletes who with plumed helmets and boots will stand *over seven feet tall.*

This is the sole sport where 200 nations and social groups can compete nightly. There might be 100 million or X00 million people in China alone watching huge Chinese charioteer-gladiator heroes Fighting for China, 100 million people in India tensely watching huge Indian charioteer heroes Fighting for India, 100 million people watching in Europe and 100 million people watching in North and South America. **O BEHOLD! O The World's Great Raceway!**, outside Las Vegas can be open 365 days a year.

How all the Team Development Groups Obtain Commercial Sponsors

The League office, in Miami or Nevada for tax reasons, will use Team Development Groups (TDG) dues to hire a sports marketing office to be there for the teams.

Team Development Groups are required to have at least one woman on the board of directors.

Sports marketing firms may be able to obtain the sponsors for the teams.

The theme: The greatest sports league ever with *the greatest advertising vehicles ever* is coming.... Inexpensive TV time...

In Summation

Dozens of nations and cities and university alumni and leading family and celebrity-owned teams can compete nightly and weekly in the League's wild, combat-sport version of 4-horse chariot racing. The League offers extraordinarily exciting television for every TV 'footprint' worldwide.

How the League Office will Get 1,000 Chariots Available

Hollywood motion picture vehicle prop makers may be a good place for the League to start. Hollywood vehicle makers can make anything, from Batmobiles to the chariots made for Ben-Hur. The League will commission many prototypes. One litmus test, Might Steve Jobs have responded to a chariot's appearance, "That's beautiful"?

Each chariot-maker is an independent entrepreneur.

The League will invite each chariot maker to have advertising pages on the League Internet site, with customer ratings.

The League will hire one or more full-time Engineer Executives to assist the Team Development Groups with chariot matters.

There is room for specialists. In chariot hitches. Wheels cannot use any rubber or metal, except perhaps the axle, and must look variously 'Ancient Roman'. Spokes-per-wheel will be limited in number, perhaps ten spokes of minimum one-inch in diameter each. See the motion picture Ben-Hur. Electrical system. Batteries. Lighting. Space under the floor for handicapping lead weights to be placed.

Every chariot must have the noted five, streaming video cameras.

Celebrities World 4-Horse Chariot Racing League can supply **2,000 hours a year of compelling worldwide television, six hours a day, 365 days**.

Celebrities World 4-Horse Chariot Racing League stands to be more exciting than two great sports, NFL football and NBA basketball, because of the wild, wheel-to-wheel whipping duels between huge male charioteer-gladiators. In comparison, NFL Football is a girly-man sport. We recommend not saying this to any NFL players. Especially Ray Lewis. That might not turn out well.

The size of the TV business for Celebrities World 4-Horse Chariot Racing League can be as if the game of soccer/football did not exist and was invented by you. You could arrange to own significant equity in *all* soccer TV worldwide.

Now, 'whipping' is not a nice word. Nor is bodychecking nor slamming up against the boards nor fistfights in hockey. Nor brutally tackling a wide receiver who has leaped up to catch the ball in NFL football. Nor the bench-clearing brawls of baseball. But within the confines and rules of a sporting contest they work.

A sample, signature event is: Fifteen 4-horse teams in a race, 60 horses charging pell-mell around the track. Say that a

German team and a Japanese team happen to be either side of a British team called Rule Britannia!. The German and Japanese team charioteers whip wildly at the British team charioteer. The British team charioteer heroically lashes back at both of them, first to one side, then to the other. This Mano a Mano is being watched in every pub in Britain, and Germany, and Japan.

The paired, power announcers shout: "Team Japanese Bullet Train and team Germany Over All!, come crashing down on Rule Britannia! and Rule Britannia! heroically fights back! It's brutal out there!"

Result: British TV fans may be shouting all over Britain, wild with excitement, and awaiting a race where Britain will not be in the middle of two other teams. Next time maybe the Japanese Bullet Train team will be in the middle of two teams, one of them Rule Britannia!

The Significance of the League Structure

The League is not just a bunch of chariots racing around. There is a league format with a 12-month cumulative points-standings and the annual World Cup Tournament. Points standings for the team (one chariot plus 4 horses, and spares for both).

Each World 4-Horse Chariot Racing League team receives, for example, 15 points for each first place finish, 14 points for second, 13 points for third down to 1 point for last place.

The same points-structure can be maintained separately for charioteers. Cumulative for each year. And cumulative for a charioteer's career. Sort of like in NBA basketball.

These point standings can be pointed out by the TV announcers. Thus, fans can follow the standings of their favorite teams and favorite charioteers.

Celebrities World 4-Horse Chariot Racing League may become the greatest sports league ever, nightly on worldwide television.

The End of this Draft for double-full-page ads in the world's major financial newspapers.

The above-noted offers a treasure trove of material for You-Tube and Facebook and Twitter entrants in the opportunity to apply for very large awards that might be paid out. Fun Disruptor Awards Chapter Thirty.

Fun Disruptor Chapter Thirty

Another Currency-Validation by World Treasury Bank MAiN that Pleases People

This is How Billionaires Can Be Acclaimed Worldwide for Decades by Popular, Liberating Actions from World Treasury Bank, the MAiN, and its Founders.

Readers Might Potentially Get Multi-Million Dollar Awards.

Unique, Speculative, Large Money Awards That Might Happen

Your Application To Become a Multi-Millionaire is Due Soon

The World Treasury Bank Plan herein intends to pay out substantial, U.S. dollar award payments to some individuals, and firms, that are able to bring this book and its plan to one or more Major Players in finance and business. The idea is that sometime after the World Treasury Bank IPO, if there is one, the Bank corporation intends to pay out anywhere from a million U.S. dollars to many millions to even nine-figures or a even a billion dollars.

Of course, a sensible response is that this unprecedented plan is unlikely to be realized. If that is your thought, you are right for you. Go with what you believe.

Nevertheless, the idea is that a person or firm that has access to one or more Major Players might send a copy of this book to the Major Player with a note, "If you happen to choose to become involved in World Treasury Bank MAiN, please see fit to mention me/us with reference to the Unusual, Speculative, Large Money Awards That Might Happen, Fun Disruptor Chapter Thirty."

Other persons who might see fit to contact one or more Major Players might be chief executive officers or publishers or editors of major financial or news publications.

Moreover, a firm that holds financial sector conferences, and might have connections to one or more Major Players, could send the book to one or more or many individuals with a cover note as described above.

Additionally, a corporation that acts as the above suggests, might decide to participate with the Major Players.

Other persons who may be able to successfully approach a Major Player could be such as: administrative assistants. Colleagues. Friends. Colleagues who might themselves be worth nine-figures or more. Relatives. Romantic friends.

The intention is to include in the offer fully 1,000, Two Million Dollar Awards. ("Make me a millionaire after taxes.")

A Major Player could have this book sent to one or more major figures in finance per week, including such as seen on the lists of the world's richest, and thereby please the world as described herein. Such Major Players might become triple-digit billionaires. Fun Disruptor Chapter Eight.

The Money Awards that May Appeal Even to Major Players

The Ten Famous Potential Enrichments are to go to, if paid, persons who know a major player and who simply bring the plan, that is, this book, to the attention of a major player.

At some point the latter major player simply says, "Name-of-Person put me onto this World Treasury Bank plan, and this had to do with why I became involved."

Then, you can apply for the First of the Ten Famous Potential Enrichments, and perhaps be moved down to one of the others. Or to No, nothing. Be aggressive. State your case. Go for the top. Get disappointed.

First Famous Potential Enrichment: One billion U.S. dollars.

Second Famous Potential Enrichment: Nine hundred million U.S. dollars

Third Famous Potential Enrichment: Eight hundred million U.S. dollars.

Fourth Famous Potential Enrichment: Seven hundred million U.S. dollars.

Fifth Famous Potential Enrichment: Six hundred million U.S. dollars.

Sixth Famous Potential Enrichment: Five hundred million U.S. dollars.

Seventh Famous Potential Enrichment: Four hundred million U.S. dollars.

Eighth Famous Potential Enrichment: Three hundred million U.S. dollars.

Ninth Famous Potential Enrichment: Two hundred million U.S. dollars.

Tenth Famous Potential Enrichment: a lousy One hundred million U.S. dollars.

TOTAL Potential Enrichment seen here is $5,500,000,000. Five and a half billion dollars. This can be compared to the equally-speculative note where it is suggested that the nature of a World Treasury Bank IPO is that it might be able to be the largest IPO ever. The largest to date, a Chinese bank, for just under $25 Billion.
THEN: World Treasury Bank MAiN may become very rich. Or not.

It *might* be that after the Initial Public Offering, soon after, or a year or two after, World Treasury Bank may be judged by Wall Street to be an extraordinarily valuable corporation. Your application may still be viable. World Treasury Bank MAiN may become worth triple-digit billions of dollars. (Chapter Eight). Then, paying out over five billion dollars in awards seems reasonable.
Decision of the judges is final, though there can be an Appeal. "Aw, come on!"

For obvious reasons, these awards are not and cannot be a promise. Throughout this section, and in this book, there are, and can be, no legal promises, not explicit or implied or assumed. You may put forward effort, sweat and tears, and get nothing. Partial awards or zero awards may be paid out. There cannot be any promises herein because the plan to get a World Treasury Bank Initial Public Offering, and the hope for a very large Wall Street valuation, is merely a plan, it is speculation, not a guarantee or anything like it.

The above-noted awards references themselves offer a treasure trove of material for YouTube and Facebook and Twitter entrants in the opportunity to apply for these very large awards that might be paid out. Yes, you can apply for an Award by referring to your YouTube facts and figures, and/or Twitter followers, and Facebook likes. Maybe try to build a YouTube channel.

Is World Treasury Bank MAiN perhaps "**The Next Big Thing**"?

Is World Treasury Bank MAiN potentially larger than Apple in Wall Street valuation, and worldwide popular enthusiasm? What do you think?

Is this modest volume perhaps the major business book ever written? Just a thought, not a claim.

Will World Treasury Bank MAiN be The Greatest Business Achievement Ever? You decide.

One Major Player can be THE MOVER, who informs other Major Players of the opportunity, and thereby becomes a historic Business Leader worldwide, written of 100 years from now. Or two or three Major Players, THE MOVERS.

A Major Player could send this book, **Private Equity Can: Make the Largest Fortunes Ever & Billions of People Happy**, available inexpensively on Amazon.com, to one or more other Major Players and ask, Please let me know if you are interested in one or more of:

1. World Treasury Bank MAiN, with free download of the private-sector, online-only, currency the MAiN to 2 Billion to 3 Billion smartphone owners worldwide.

2. The Walking-Talking Robots Convention. Might Walking-Talking Robots someday become as large as the automobile business worldwide?

3. The World Parliament of Women, with two to three billion women worldwide voting by Internet.

4. Might Celebrities World 4-Horse Chariot Racing League with 150 nations competing nightly become as large as all of TV sports worldwide?

5. The free, streaming university for all human beings forever achievement, World Treasury Bank MAiN University.

Private Equity Can: Make the Largest Fortunes Ever & Billions of People Happy is Copyright 2013 by Terrence McCloy, Beverly Hills, CA.

The Following Are Each and All Trademarks

World Treasury Bank. MAiN. MAiNPay. Sellers Planet. MAiNMessage. MAiNCall. MAiNChat. World Treasury Bank Global Stock Exchange. World Walking-Talking Robot Makers Convention. World Parliament of Women. Her-Phalanx. The Women-Only Gates onto The Great Gold Circle. The Emancipation Proclamation for All Women Worldwide. The Eternal Hand-held Candle Flame. School Professors Guild. Celebrities World 4-Horse Chariot Racing League. O BEHOLD! O The World's Great Raceway!. Flat-side-Infinite Loop Raceway. Global Giants League. 1,000 Year Immortals Cup. The Forum of the 12 Caesars Raceway. Ben-Hur Raceway. The Raceway of the 100 Nations. Asia's World Tourist Raceway. Rio's World Raceway Park. Australia's 100 Nations Raceway. The World Show of Shows Raceway. Televised Sports Entertainment Group. Chariots Licensing Properties Corporation. Chariots Raceway Management Corporation. Chariots as a fashion/lifestyle trademark. Chariots/The Neighborhood Pub/Club/Sports Bar. Universe Cup Tournament. Champion of All Champions. The League of Leading Families. Judgment Day. Global Super Champion. The Champion of All Champions. Emperor Caesar for a Year "Bestrides the World Like a Colossus". Global Victory. Great Gold Chalice Cup. Empress of the World for a Year. 1,000 Year Immortals Cup. Suuuper!Party!, and the stylized horses as seen in the Apollo Fountains at Versailles, are each Trademarks of GreatBuncha, Terrence McCloy.

Major Players, in the U.S. and abroad, are herewith invited to communicate with Terrence in Complete Confidentiality.

Terrence McCloy, Beverly Hills, California. Will Travel. Let's Meet.

Email: wtbterrence@gmail.com

Twitter: @wtbterrence

ABOUT THE AUTHOR

Terrence McCloy is a former screenwriter, Oscar-nominated. He has a long-time interest in disruptor business models. He chills out by riding horseback in the hills of Malibu.

www.ingramcontent.com/pod-product-compliance
Lightning Source LLC
Chambersburg PA
CBHW051443170526
45166CB00001B/94